VERBAL ABUSE

Verbal Abuse

Grace H. Ketterman, M.D.

Servant Publications
Ann Arbor, Michigan

128853

Vine Books is an imprint of Servant Publications especially designed to serve Evangelical Christians.

Published by Servant Publications
P.O. Box 8617
Ann Arbor, Michigan 48107

Cover design by Michael Andaloro

92 93 94 95 96 10 9 8 7 6 5 4 3 2

Printed in the United States of America

ISBN 0-89283-736-5

Library of Congress Cataloging-in-Publication Data
Ketterman, Grace H.
Verbal abuse : healing the hidden wound / Grace H. Ketterman.
p. cm.
Includes bibliographical references.
ISBN 0-89283-736-5
1. Criticism, Personal. 2. Invective. I. Title.
BF637.C74K48 1992
158'.2—dc20   91–46623

Contents

Introduction

ARE YOU THE VICTIM OF VERBAL ABUSE? From my counseling experience, I know the wounds are many and the pain is very deep. You have shown the willingness to examine this issue in your own life by picking up this book. While there may be little you can actually do to change your abuser, there is much you can learn about how to stop absorbing such hurtful words as truth. You can learn to eradicate their power over you.

In the pages that follow, we will first try to examine just what defines verbal abuse—a challenging goal in itself. Then we will see how these ugly words insidiously insert themselves into our relationships at home, at school, at work, in our everyday social contacts, and even at church. The many and varied forms of verbal abuse can be quite subtle but nonetheless damaging. The effects are permanent and often life-shaping.

After we have examined the various forms and effects of verbal abuse, you will be faced with some difficult questions about how abuse operates in your own life. Do you feel trapped in an abusive situation? Do you threaten to walk away and then remain? Do you unwittingly invite abuse or perpetuate this vicious cycle by your own behavior? Apart from a change in your abuser, what can *you* do to change or break that cycle? How can you confront your abuser in a healthy way?

Perhaps you were the victim of verbal abuse during your childhood. Perhaps you suffered abuse in relationships that are no longer part of your life. Learning how to heal the hurts of the past is a complex process, but one that is certainly possible. That healing will require commitment on your part coupled with perseverance. You will need deep courage to reopen old wounds and relive the pain, along with utter honesty to examine your own role in an abusive relationship.

To help you to apply these insights to your own life experience, I have concluded each chapter with several questions for personal reflection. You may find it helpful to write out your answers on a separate sheet of paper. The effort you expend in probing more deeply into this issue of verbal abuse will hopefully repay invaluable dividends in future peace, joy, and success. You no longer need to remain a victim. You *can* experience healing and freedom from the emotional damage of verbal abuse. You *can* break through to forgiveness and release.

While the focus of this book is most clearly aimed at the cessation of your being a victim and at your own healing, you will see how often victims of abuse become abusers themselves. The awful question must be faced: *have you become an abuser yourself?* You may experience a great deal of shame and guilt over your powerlessness to overcome habits of abuse toward those you deeply love. You need to learn how to cope with the pain within yourself as the victim of cruel words, while at the same time learning how to break the vicious cycle in your own unhealthy ways of relating.

Such a task is indeed daunting! Support in this area is crucial if you are to work through the resentment, anger, and bitterness so common to victims of verbal abuse. I encourage you to find a trusted friend with whom you can share this painful journey. Professional counseling can also make your efforts more productive in working through the emotional issues surrounding verbal abuse.

Joining a support group of others who understand the deep emotional pain inflicted by abusive words can also be a very great help. I have included an appendix with guidelines for using this book in a twelve-week support group for victims of verbal abuse. Is such a support group available in your area? If not, could you be instrumental in starting one yourself? Perhaps an important part of your own healing will be reaching out to help others who have suffered the same kind of pain.

Open your heart to God. He cares deeply for you and wants to touch the hidden hurts in your life. Let his words of loving kindness and mercy sink into your spirit and be a healing salve for your wounds. As you let go of your pain, your heavenly Father will fill you instead with the joy of being loved.

ONE

What Is Verbal Abuse?

*"Sticks and stones may break my bones,
but words can never hurt me."*

✦ ✦ ✦

Beth's sparkling brown eyes grew somber. Could what her mother said about her be true? "Your sister can make her living by her brains, but you will have to make it in life by your hands." Was she really less intelligent than her younger sister? Hadn't they scrapped and played together? Studied and worked together? But the powerful words of her mother had been seared into the very core of this young girl's beliefs.

In the years that followed, Beth still did not give up easily on her academic pursuits. She continued to study hard and compete with her sister for top grades in biology—and often won! But in the end, Beth decided to major in business and typing. The words her mother had prophesied in a disparaging way were fulfilled in her daughter's career as a secretary.

In fact, Beth's professional life is highly successful. Her career as a secretary and eventually office manager is one of great dignity and respect, and one which uses lots of brain power as well as nimble fingers. The important point is that Beth's decision was profoundly influenced by her mother's pronouncement, based on mistaken perceptions and spoken in a derogatory way. Because of the lack of respect shown by her mother, Beth continued to struggle with feelings of inferiority most of her life, even though her contributions at work were of great value.

Many other forces had undoubtedly contributed to this woman's decisions and career direction, but her mother's words in particular had been a major guiding factor in Beth's life. Who can know the pain those words of *comparison* inflicted on a young girl's heart? And who can measure the unnecessary restrictions they may have imposed on her development and career?

That "words can never hurt" is simply not true! Cruel names and labels *can* hurt us—dreadfully! Many times the emotional damage is unintentional. Crippling comments may seem so trivial to the speaker as to be soon forgotten. But at a crucial moment or from an important person, certain words spoken to a vulnerable, receptive individual can make or break a life.

Words can indeed be abusive and result in emotional damage. Many of us have experiences that verify the fact. But a formal definition of verbal abuse is actually very difficult to establish. I have sat in committees for hours trying to formulate statements that could be useful in such an effort. In order to protect victims and stop the abuse, such a clarification would be most helpful!

Here are seven ingredients of verbal abuse that I have gleaned through my own experiences.

1. Verbal abuse causes emotional damage because of the victim's sense of *rejection* of his or her value as a person.
2. Verbal abuse may *isolate* its victim from social activities

and friendships by destroying the self-esteem required for such relationships.

3. Verbal abuse creates *terror* in the victim. The fear that he or she is worthless destroys hope for the future.

4. Verbal abuse *ignores the basic needs* of its victims. Everyone has three basic emotional needs: unconditional acceptance, approval, and consistency. The victim of ongoing verbal abuse knows only the last of these, and then only in an emotionally damaging way.

5. Verbal abuse may *corrupt the values and behaviors* of the victim through the use of vulgar language and crude accusations. One young woman told me, "My father accused me so often of being a whore that I decided I might as well be one!"

6. Verbal abuse *degrades* victims by robbing them of self-esteem.

7. Verbal abuse *exploits* its victim for the benefits of the abuser, especially from a temporary sense of power—false as it is—unleashed during the abusive tirade.

HIDDEN SCARS

Verbal abuse very likely accompanies physical abuse. The latter is easily defined and often clearly provable. Bruises and black eyes demonstrate the damage inflicted by physical abuse. But many authorities believe verbal abuse is more damaging to the very soul of its victim than is physical abuse to the body. In 1986, Bailey and Bailey wrote, "It is highly likely that emotional maltreatment precedes other forms of abuse or neglect" (see Bibliography).

I have chosen not to deal with physical abuse in this book. Despite the profound importance of that topic, the more difficult area of verbal abuse has been neglected and thus will be our focus throughout these pages. Here is a very simple but useful definition of this complex issue: *"Verbal abuse is any statement to a victim that results in emotional damage. Such damage limits his or her happiness and productivity for a lifetime" (Adapted from philosophies of the Metro Task Force on Emotional Abuse/Neglect. Kansas City, Missouri, 1987).*

In essence, verbal abuse creates emotional scars that may permanently disfigure a person. But to avoid any sense of hopelessness, let me briefly discuss scars as a medical phenomenon. Scars result from damage to normal, healthy tissue. They are nature's method of knitting together body tissues that have been severed or injured in some way. Once that knitting process has been completed, scars continue to offer some measure of protection because they are tougher and harder to damage than normal tissue.

Emotional scars, while leaving a permanent mark on the soul, can also serve a useful purpose. They are reminders of the lessons we can learn from painful experiences. They are symbols of a healthy toughness we can acquire, once we understand verbal abuse. Our emotional scars remind us to learn and use greater control over our feelings and how we react to abuse from others. That sense of self-control is, after all, what we all have. We can rarely, if ever, control others. But we can always decide how we respond to them!

The tragedy of abuse is its repetitive pattern through succeeding generations and over a broad range of life situations. Children who were verbally abused are more than likely to abuse their peers, siblings, and teachers. As they mature, they will probably abuse their spouses, fellow employees, or bosses. If these victims are in a position of authority, they will no doubt abuse those whom they supervise. And heaven help their own children!

Few, if any, abusers set out in the morning to abuse anyone! They are generally bright and fine folks. But mounting stress and building tension finally reach a breaking point. Sooner or later, the old mechanisms go to work, and the familiar, devastating patterns of abuse are once again repeated.

Once people have verbally exploded, they usually attempt to justify themselves by various mental defenses. "I was only being honest and open!" "I said that for her own good. She has to learn!" "I was only kidding! Can't he take a joke?" "If she is that sensitive, it's certainly not my fault!" And the inevitable, "It's his problem! I was only being frank!" Any and all of these beliefs can seem to excuse verbal cruelty. But, of course, even while they harden the conscience of the perpetrators, such excuses fail to alleviate the pain of the victims.

This book will clarify what constitutes verbal abuse in a variety of life situations. It will discuss why and how abusive patterns develop—how you, too, could be an abuser. And best of all, it will focus on how you can be healed of the toxins of your past abuse, how you can stop taking any more abuse from others, as well as how you can break any abusive habits you yourself may have developed.

✦ ✦ ✦

Study Questions

1. What specific childhood names and labels or other derogatory words were especially hurtful to you? Did you ever bravely answer someone's stinging words with "sticks and stones may break my bones, but words can never hurt me?" Can you now recognize the lasting emotional damage and scars produced by such cruel words?

2. Describe any disparaging words that may have pushed you in certain directions academically or professionally.

3. How do you see these seven ingredients of verbal abuse operating in your own life?

   a. produces a sense of rejection

   b. produces isolation

   c. produces a sense of terror and worthlessness

   d. ignores basic needs of unconditional acceptance, approval, and consistency

   e. degrades its victims by robbing them of self-esteem

   f. exploits its victims for benefit of abuser

4. How would you define verbal abuse?

Part One

Verbal Abuse in the Family

TWO

Behind Closed Doors

✦ ✦ ✦

T HE FAMILY IS SUPPOSED TO BE a haven, a place of safety in a heartless and increasingly frightening world. Yet, all too commonly, home has become a private world of horror—the safe place to explode one's frustrations, shredding the emotions of those unfortunate enough to be there. Few relationships absorb as much chronic abuse as marriage.

Verbal abuse is in part an expression of personal inadequacy. In the stressful arena of one's job, only a few individuals have much power. Employees take abuse from others in order to keep their jobs and maintain the appearance of strength. But at home, these same victims can displace their fears and inflict the accompanying anger upon those who have even less power than they do. Doing so usually produces a feeling of power. And when family members react in fear and trembling, that false power is exaggerated. So the vicious cycle is established.

ROOTED IN THE PAST

The inner weaknesses that predispose people to such a vicious cycle have their taproots in the past. That certainly was true of Fred and Gladys.

"You are exactly like your mother!" Fred pronounced. "You used to tell me what a martyr she was and how you hated that, but you're just like her!"

For what seemed like the thousandth time that month, Gladys yelled back, "Fred, that's not true and it's certainly not fair! It's just that you are so mean. Your mother has told me how cruel your father was, and I can see you're just like him. It's no wonder I cry! I can't ever please you and in your eyes, you're always the one who is right!" Once again, Gladys helplessly dissolved in tears and her angry husband felt that he had won the dispute. He had verbally overpowered his wife.

Every marriage contains areas of disagreement between spouses. These usually have as their core some sort of *power struggle*—the intense need on the part of both husband and wife to prove strength. In order to win a fight, one or both spouses tend to resort to unfair tactics. Such arguments inevitably include verbal abuse. Sooner or later, one will make statements that pierce like arrows into the very soul of the other. In the emotional anguish of the moment, the injured one often impulsively retaliates.

From such simple beginnings, the pain of broken trust and often broken marriages is born. Verbal abuse in marriage is the negative skill of discovering and needlessly injuring the tender, vulnerable spots in one's partner—all in the service of unconsciously trying to prove one's own power. Certainly to facilitate growth in the object of one's love, there are times when painful, critical truth must be stated. Such corrections, however, can be effected lovingly and with concern, rather than in retaliation and pain.

Let me give an example from my own early marriage. I had become friends with a fellow medical student who could make us all laugh. The study of medicine produces tremendous stress, so to be able to cut loose and laugh was a rare and refreshing gift. This woman's humor, however, also carried a flavor of cynicism that became caustic. All too often, her sharp wit cruelly sacrificed the personal dignity of others.

Because I enjoyed the laughter, I gradually learned to copy my friend's humor. Being able to make others laugh became a source of pride. My husband, however, was aware of the basic cruelty masked by this particular sort of humor. He waited until I had made a joke at the expense of a friend. Then in private, he reviewed the episode with me and asked if I had noticed the confusion and hurt of the target of that particular joke.

My husband gently interpreted what he had observed in my friend and reassured me that such cruelty was foreign to my gentler nature. He lovingly offered to help me stop this new habit of damaging humor. Speaking the truth in love is a major preventive of verbal abuse. You, too, can learn this loving art!

SEEDS OF TRUTH

Let's return to our earlier example to clarify the issue of verbal abuse through criticizing one's in-laws. Such abuse usually has its taproot in rivalry. Fred criticized his wife through finding fault with her mother. Two very significant things were wrong with that. First, Gladys had often been hurt by her mother's "poor me" attitude and had vowed she would never practice such behavior. To admit she was behaving in the same way would be owning a major failure. Gladys naturally recoiled from such an admission. Second, Fred's condemnation of Gladys and her mother contained the element of making his family seem superior to hers.

This example also clarifies the fact that most abuse derives its power from the seeds of truth that it contains. Gladys often played the martyr role she so disliked, but was unable to face that fact for years. Eventually, Gladys not only recognized her fault but was also able to correct it. Verbal abuse needs to be examined for any validity it may contain and corrections made accordingly.

Over twenty years ago, Dr. Thomas Harris wrote a book entitled, *I'm OK—You're OK*, in which he described four major life positions each individual assumes in relationships with another. Although this "value free" approach has definite limitations, these four possible positions offer some helpful insights:

1. I'm okay, you're not.
2. You're okay, I'm not.
3. Neither of us is okay.
4. I'm okay, you're okay.

You can readily see the first three relationships cannot be positive, healthy ones. Only the fourth offers the possibility of respect, joy, and healthy intimacy. Both Fred and Gladys resorted to competition for the number one spot in their marriage. On the surface, of course, Fred wanted his wife to stop crying and feeling sorry for herself. Gladys, in turn, was saying underneath, "If only you wouldn't be so mean, I could be different."

Neither is likely to change as long as the blame can so obviously be placed on the other. And neither can feel really good about him/herself or the other as long as the abuse and insults continue. Fred and Gladys can begin to change by learning unconditional acceptance of themselves and each other. Only in the safety of such a secure family environment can faults be most readily faced, and growth and change take place.

THE WEAPON OF RIDICULE

Blazing with anger only moments earlier, George was now laughing in merriment. "What's the matter, Helen?" he asked. "Can't you take a joke?" Her downcast face slowly brightened as she tried to laugh. She would show her husband she could be a good sport and "take a joke."

Later, however, Helen had time to review not only this current episode but countless similar ones in the past six years of their marriage. She tried to justify her husband's verbal ridicule. Perhaps he was just hung over from a bad day at work when he criticized the dinner she had prepared. But on too many other occasions, George had disapproved of an outfit she wore to work, or pointed out the fact that her girlish curves were becoming a bit too matronly.

It was true! George did express many of his criticisms in an unbearably abusive way. "Have you considered joining the circus as the fat lady?" he might ask. Or, "What did you do, raid the neighbor's garbage for dinner?" Funny? Not very. In fact, not at all funny.

George would often point out his wife's shortcomings with the focused pain of a stiletto. How well he knew the tender spots in her personality that were vulnerable to his verbal stabs. He also learned that she could not resist reacting to his attacks. And George had discovered long before to avoid feeling guilty about his habit by ending the interaction with, "What's the matter with you? Can't you take a joke?"

This man had learned as a child that he could often avert his father's anger and his mother's tears by claiming his remarks were only in jest. His technique worked equally well on his brothers and sisters, and so this negative skill quickly became a habit. George refused to admit—perhaps even to himself—that he played such an unfair and damaging game.

As Helen began to understand her husband, she had to face the painful truth. She was married to an abusive man. And she had encouraged his abuse by joining in the laughter at her own expense. It took a great deal of courage and immense tenacity, but Helen began a campaign to stem the flow of hurtful words. "No more caustic humor, George. Tell me simply, 'I'd love to have no more casseroles for dinner. I just don't like them, but I do enjoy pork chops,'" she instructed. When he reverted to old habits, Helen ignored them and refused to try to laugh her way out of the pain.

Slowly George's habits changed, but in the many months I knew them, Helen never totally mastered the art of refusing to take his jabs. She was honest enough to care what he thought and independent enough to react in self-defense. She was not, however, mature enough to realize that he attacked her because he needed to feel powerful.

Later, we will discuss in more detail what you as a victim can do to stop being abused. There may be little you can actually do to stop your abuser, but there is much you can do to help you stop absorbing those hurtful words as the truth. You can eradicate their power over you!

DRAMATIC DIFFERENCES

As a college freshman I wrote a paper on friendship. One of the values high on my list of priorities in a friend was basic agreement on various issues. My wise, mature professor liked most of my ideas, but on that topic she responded, "Perhaps you should consider the ability to disagree, agreeably!"

Over the years, I have learned for myself the truth of her wisdom. Unfortunately, that was not true of Howard and Debbie. Their marriage was in serious difficulty, and much of their trouble was due to verbal abuse. Their pattern of abuse focused on each one's very different set of values. Debbie loved elegance and perfection. Her house and personal appearance evidenced her meticulous care. Classical music was always heard in her home and she maintained season tickets to the nearest symphony concerts. Her grammar was flawless, and Debbie knew a great deal about classic literature and art.

Howard's lifestyle exemplified the reverse of most of these values. He loved the outdoors and found it a chore to remove his muddy boots outside the kitchen door. His truck radio blared the twang of country rhythm. Howard was comfortable only when the newspaper was strewn about his easy chair. His favorite TV shows were from the era of "Hee-Haw" and "The Dukes of Hazzard." It was a major pain for him to don a necktie and he owned only one dress shirt.

How these two ever married may seem a mystery, but this example focuses on one of the common reasons for verbal abuse. Both Howard and Debbie felt very insecure. Debbie had been attracted by Howard's manliness, and he in turn felt the need to be accepted by higher-brow folks. Debbie actually loved the strength of Howard's outdoor interests; he admired her daintiness. But each came to feel inferior to the other in certain aspects of their lives. Debbie began to feel weak and frail and wished she were stronger. Howard often felt awkward and envied Debbie's friends who could wear black ties and converse comfortably at social events.

Their differences were dramatic. The tragedy was the way in which each used the other's values to inflict unbelievable insults. With only a roll of her eyes, Debbie could express her disgust of Howard, but she rarely stopped at such body language. Instead, she regularly apologized to her friends for Howard's "low taste" and "slovenly appearance." She often commented to him about his "rural background" and his "uneducated family." Howard, not to be outdone, retaliated in fine style. He told her clearly that she was a "snob" and that she must be a "phoney" to pretend she was so smart. He knew what she really was like.

In their attempt to feel better about themselves, they derogated each other. At the time he heaved those verbal stones at Debbie, Howard felt powerful. And the only way she knew to protect herself from the pain of those attacks was to hurl them back. As their inflicted pain increased, layer by layer, so did the emotional callouses they wore.

Somehow their marriage stayed together, perhaps because each needed the abuse of the other to punish some long-forgotten sins. Finally, the pain pierced even their calloused hearts and forced them to seek the help they so sorely needed.

RELIGIOUS SLINGSHOTS

"All you ever do anymore is go to church!" Jim complained. "What's the Reverend got that I haven't?" His wife, Bev, was indeed a regular attendant at the services in her church. For her the benefits of such a practice were multiple. She was able to express her love for God freely. Spiritual growth offered her a sense of peace and strength. Bev had found new friends in her church. And she did see in the pastor a role model of the father she had never had.

Jim's accusation and obvious disapproval created not only pain but confusion. Could he actually be jealous? Should she give up the practice of her faith to please her husband? Why wouldn't he join her?

Communicating about such personal and profound issues as religious beliefs can be almost impossible. Yet, differences in this sensitive area of life are extremely common. Accusations like Jim's can easily arise out of guilt feelings and insecurity. Uncertainty and shyness produce the reticence to reply. Like Bev, many a spouse remains silent, deeply pained.

Religious differences are many and varied. From agnosticism to faith, historic family roots in a particular church tradition may oppose a very different set of beliefs in one's partner. The countless disagreements in any marriage can center around a myriad of variations in values, interpretations, personality, preferences, and political issues. Religion, unfortunately, is one of the most common arenas of conflict.

It is important to realize this is not completely the fault of religious differences. Many individuals stubbornly resist practicing tolerance and unconditional acceptance in the area of faith. Instead they often try to force their partners to embrace their own beliefs. Tragically, such attempts can be so emotionally laden that pain is easily inflicted. By its very nature, such pain defeats even the most well intentioned efforts to convince the loved one to share the values of faith.

We can see the painful words growing out of an unconscious sense of powerlessness—and in Jim's case, a deep fear of abandonment. What if Bev no longer loved him? What if her church, her pastor, her activities, her new friends, crowded him out? Jim felt coerced to set up a win-lose struggle to find out if his wife really loved him. How sad that he didn't understand the principle of everyone winning. If only he could have at least explored the benefits of Bev's spiritual world, instead of feeling so threatened.

COMMON DISAGREEMENTS

Three avenues most commonly traveled by marriage partners fundamentally reveal power struggles—the attempt to prove that one is right and the other is wrong. These disagreements are often prompted by an inner insecurity and a deep need to prove personal worth. Usually grounded in long standing habits of fighting over particular issues, these patterns are difficult to change. Indeed, rarely are the combatants even aware of the futile war that is going on day after day. They may experience only a vague compulsion to force the opponent to give in, thereby proving they themselves are right.

Money. Few issues are as symbolic of power as money. In marriage, accusations and blame centering around this matter are frequent, often true, and always painful. "You're a selfish spendthrift, just like your father!" "And you're a nagging shrew exactly like your mother. I should have known you'd be like her; you always sounded like her!" "Why can't you do a simple thing like keep the checkbook balanced? You must have a streak of stupidity!" "You never consider my need for a little money of my own. All you ever think about is what you want!"

Some of these abusive words may sound all too familiar! Perhaps all of them are part of your marital dialogue. Hopefully, you will learn a new dialogue focused on love instead of power. Spouses who have suffered abuse over financial issues need to know what they can do to help stop that pain. I have found the following steps to be helpful.

1. First, you can learn to feel secure enough to give up your end of the tug-of-war. Trust your own good will, God-given worth, and the love of your spouse.
2. Next, try to understand your spouse's particular struggles. For instance, men struggle with the fear of weakness and the immense demands of our culture that they must always be strong. If a wife can recognize her husband's vulnerability, her love can help her to protect him rather than counter-attack.
3. Then you can prepare a budget that will include his or her needs as well as your own and the family's. If you can stay calm, firm, and loving, you may be surprised that your spouse will abandon verbal attacks and work through this vital area of married life with you. You, the victim, can become the winner in the battle against verbal abuse!

Children. Another natural avenue for the wreckage of verbal abuse rests on the delicate presence of little children—and bigger ones, too! In fact, it is easy to abuse your spouse, your in-laws, other relatives, and your children—all with one blow. "Have you seen what *your* stupid kid did to my electric screwdriver? He's just as careless as your dad! Can't you teach him any sense of responsibility?" "You're making a big sissy out of my son. Why must you coddle him so? Just like your mom treated your big wimp of a brother!" The words may vary slightly, but the sound is the same—a hammer of insults that attack at least three generations in one blow!

Not only do disagreements over children damage loving feelings between spouses, they are devastating to the children as well. When a daughter is insulted in such a way that her mother is also hurt, she loses her entire sense of worth and safety. She must be terrible or Daddy wouldn't say such things; Mommy must be weak or she wouldn't stand for Daddy to say such things; and Daddy is frightening in the power to hurt all of them, so she cannot respect him. The exciting truth is that such abuse can stop. We'll discuss how in Part IV of this book.

Sex. Few areas of life are as sensitive as sexual feelings. And in few ways can one experience the death knell of genuine love and desire as quickly as through attacks on one's sexuality. Men are thought to be more in need of sexual expression and identity than women. But my experience is that women share an equal need to feel desirable and fulfilled sexually.

When fights and insults have been raging in the kitchen, it is difficult to feel loving in the bedroom. Once the basic trust in one another's love is damaged, a vicious cycle is set in motion. Verbal abuse, doubt, suspicion, and the loss of physical intimacy can ultimately result in the total destruction of a marriage.

"You're worthless in bed!" Verne muttered tensely. He wanted sexual intimacy frequently and could not see why his wife was not as interested. He forgot that he had insulted Maxine's appearance, her dinner, and her housekeeping that very evening. He knew she held a job to increase their income, yet he expected her to measure up to the standards of his stay-at-home mother.

Verne felt it would be effeminate to help Maxine clean house or do laundry. That was "women's work." But he clearly felt his masculinity was expressed most superbly in love-making. He determined to show Maxine how to be sexy and tried to coerce her by insulting and belittling her. If he insulted her severely enough, he felt it would shock her into trying harder to please him.

On her side, Maxine had learned that being passive and compliant would get the requisite love-making over with, one more time. Having been hurt so often by this man, she could no longer bring herself to even care about what he wanted, much less try to please him. In fact, in subtle ways, Maxine regained just a touch of her lost dignity by refusing to act interested in his love-making.

What a tragic result of unnecessary abuse by verbal insults. The warmth, joy, and intimacy of sex were lost to both of these marriage partners because of ugly words spoken out of misunderstanding and pain. Many of you may know exactly how Maxine felt as the victim of verbal abuse focused on the sexual relationship.

We have explored the ways in which verbal abuse can wreak havoc between a husband and wife, as well as between all family members. Careless words and spiteful insults are so lethal in a marriage because of the very intimacy of the relationship. Opening oneself fully to the love of another also means being vulnerable to deep pain. And living with another human being day in and day out leaves no lack of opportunities to see the shortcomings of one's partner. We especially need God's grace to resist the ever-present temptation to lash out in verbal abuse.

Verbal abuse of any kind between parents always hurts the children as well as themselves. Children share an uncanny ability to sense tension between their parents. Even when the adults keep their disagreements and hurtful words out of hearing range, children feel the pain inflicted on their parents. Such a situation inevitably sets up a battle array that includes the entire family. Children will usually take sides with one parent and may be set at odds with their siblings as well. Verbal abuse is a tragically destructive force that endangers the very souls of everyone within range of the fallout. Don't do it!

✦ ✦ ✦

Study Questions

1. What verbally abusive arguments in your marriage have reflected a *struggle for power*? How did you *feel* when abusive statements were aimed at you by your spouse? How did you respond to your spouse? How did you express your feelings?

2. How do you identify with the unspoken lament: "If only you wouldn't be so mean, I could be different"?

3. Describe specific examples of painful ridicule passed off by your spouse as just a joke. How can you now identify those barbs as verbally abusive?

4. What different values or religious beliefs between you and your spouse have been a source of verbal abuse?

5. Describe how issues relating to money, children, and sex generate disagreements in your own marriage. Which hurt you the most?

6. In what ways has your ability to be vulnerable and intimate with your spouse been damaged by verbal abuse, whether from your childhood or more recently?

7. Can you begin to see that you may discover more power in yourself than you ever believed you had?

THREE

Young and Impressionable

✦ ✦ ✦

CARMEN BIT HER LIP AS SHE TRIED HARD NOT TO CRY. What did Grandma mean that she would be just like her mother? Mama was so pretty she would be lucky to be like her. Yet Grandma yelled at her all the time—telling her she was lazy, no good, stupid. If only Mama were home more, she thought, life would be better. But when her mother was there, Grandma yelled at her, too. This young girl did not even understand the names Grandma called her mother, but she could tell by her face that they hurt Mama very much. And so her mother stayed away a lot, having for the most part abandoned her to the mercy of her grandmother.

If only Carmen could also have run away from her grandmother's angry predictions and labels, her story may have had a happier ending. Instead, her grandfather took pity on her. He invited his "little buddy" to go fishing with him, taught her to repair motors and work with his tools. This love-starved girl found her only safety in the shadow of her grandfather.

Unfortunately, Carmen learned not only to do his tasks but to adopt his feelings and mannerisms as well. She learned to stand, walk, and talk like he did. Without realizing what was happening in the depths of her spirit, she essentially rejected her femininity because she could not tolerate the abuse and neglect of the only two women she knew. But the acceptance and warmth of Grandpa meant the world to her.

Only when Carmen reached puberty did she recognize that she was different from other girls. They would giggle and tease the boys, obviously flirting with them. Carmen had no such interests. In fact she recognized that she felt the way that young men acted—magnetically drawn to the cute teenage girls in her school.

Carmen did not want to be a lesbian, but the abuse she experienced from her grandmother was enough to make her reject the very idea of being a woman. She would not be like her! Nor could she feel good about becoming like her mother. Grandma said terrible things about Mama, and Carmen could never see why her mom so totally abandoned her. The only role model the child could find was gentle, loving Grandpa. She would be like him. And so she was.

LITTLE ONES WITH BIG EARS

Her angry voice became a piercing arrow as Carol screamed at her husband. "You're a bumbling idiot! You can't even fix my kitchen faucet without flooding my floors. You never have helped me! You always make a mess worse than the problem ever was. I don't know why I ever expect you to do anything right! All you men are stupid, incompetent fools!"

Al silently absorbed her outpoured venom. Try as he would, he could not let the piercing words fly by. After fifteen years of marriage, he had heard them so often from her—and from his mother before her. Critical, condemning, harsh words, deepening the scars he carried from early childhood. They must be true; he was clumsy and inept. But he could still sense a tiny voice within that whispered, "Hey, Al, you can do it this time!" And once in a while he could fix the leaks and breaks that so often occur in any home. What he couldn't fix was the tirade that tried his very soul when he faltered or, (God forbid!), failed.

Because he believed in the marriage commitment, Al stayed and took it. Furthermore, Carol was a beautiful woman, a great cook, and a fairly competent mother— except, of course, when she screamed at the children as she did at him. He vaguely understood that Carol's mother was a screamer, too. And he knew that his father-in-law had weathered those turbulent years until time and age had smoothed the storms to a bearable level. Yes, Al decided, I can weather these storms as well. And so he did.

What Al missed, however, was the impact of the abuse on his young son. Three-year-old Billy cowered, wide-eyed in the living room behind the sofa. Not a word of his mother's torrent did he miss. How he wished Dad would say something! Do anything! Maybe Mom was right—maybe all men are stupid, bumbling idiots.

As time wore on without his mother's running out of abusive words, Billy made a decision that grew more firm each day. He would never be like Daddy. Not him! No bumbling, stupid, incompetent man would he become. He wasn't sure what all those words meant, but he knew he didn't want Mom to think them of him.

Day after day, this sensitive, bright, and quiet lad grew more and more like Mom. He adopted her exacting habits of perfection, learned to share her skills and hobbies, walked and talked just like she did. When Billy reached puberty, he found that girls held no appeal. He was even afraid of them. He felt safer, more comfortable with males. And then he discovered that he was sexually drawn to men, not girls. Billy's masculinity had been mortally wounded—equally by his mother's words and his father's passivity.

There are many similarly wounded children who suffer from verbal abuse between their parents. Those parents generally do not *want* to hurt their children. Believe it or not, they don't even want to hurt each other! They are both caught in a web of misunderstanding, self-protection, and the pervasive, compelling need for everything to be exactly "right." Compulsively, they fall into a habit of trying to convince their partners that their ideas and ways are the only right ones. The spouse, of course, must be wrong.

Furthermore, a spouse like Carol expects her husband to meet all of her needs. After all, she chose a man who was somewhat like her dad, softspoken and patient. What she had overlooked was the fact that his patience became passivity and his quietness seemed stupid. She could not tolerate those qualities and desperately kept trying to make him change. Perhaps if she yelled louder or used more forceful words, he would hear and then he would change. She never thought those words would estrange her husband, much less damage her son!

Diane was another vulnerable child. Night after night she covered her ears with her big, soft pillow. But it only muffled her parents' fights without stopping them. This little girl finally became resigned to the fact that they would argue and disagree. They fought over money, sex, and the children in turn. Diane was left feeling guilty and desperately afraid they would divorce. Sometimes she wished they would. She vowed she would not marry a man who yelled at her as Dad raged at Mom.

Indeed, Diane married a man who was always ready to give in to her wishes. Not only did Chad never yell, he often withdrew in an icy politeness that shut her out completely. She remembered her parents' verbal abuse and wondered if that might be preferable after all to the coldness she endured from her own husband. Over the years, Diane's parents had endured the abuse between them and found some uneasy peace. But the scars their angry words had etched in their daughter's personality still exist, handicapping her in her own marital adjustment.

TRAINING OR GOADING?

Dale glared in defiance as I described to him some problems his young daughter was evidencing. Evvie was alternately withdrawn and sullen or aggressive and rude. It seemed likely that she was enduring some abuse and was either frightened or angry. As I questioned Dale about his discipline and training methods, he became extremely defensive.

He told me angrily that, of course, he yelled at Evvie. She was just lazy and stubborn, and he wanted her to know she would never make it in life with such stupidity. Furthermore, this distraught father told his daughter these facts nearly every day, but he elaborated extensively when she brought home her report card. If Evvie dared to speak up to explain that she didn't understand decimals in math, he yelled, "There you go again, making excuses! You're stupid and lazy. You don't even try." So this young girl finally gave up trying and fulfilled her father's prophecy about laziness and stupidity.

Then I asked Dale, "And how did your parents try to get you to succeed in school?" He became irate. "There you go again! All you psychiatrists try to blame kids' problems on their parents and grandparents. My dad yelled at me and it worked! I've made a success of my life! And Evvie will have to do the same!" What a tragedy! Two generations of people, marred and limited by verbal abuse, and not even able, at first, to see the damage.

Brad shuffled his feet uneasily and glued his gaze to the

floor. His face tightened as if to prevent a single tear from revealing his pain. Once again, he had done it—gotten into a fight. Over the course of several weeks, Brad and his parents had been seeing me for help with his habit of hitting whenever he became angry. He was, at heart, a tender lad who felt immense remorse after a fight. But he was also sensitive and impulsive. When anyone called him names or made fun of him, Brad felt it was his duty to defend himself by getting even.

On this particular day, his parents were finally facing their role in these problems. His mother discussed her habit of nagging him about many aspects of his life, attempting to help him become the perfect son she hoped he would be. She could see how her constant picking at him fed his store of anger. And then came the words that helped steer Brad's life along a dangerous road: "I'm just so afraid he'll become like his Uncle Tony. Tony is my brother, and he's in prison for ten years for beating up a guy in a fight!"

We quickly discovered that Brad looked a lot like Tony, had many of the same personality traits, and actually acted much like him. Brad's mother had lived with the constant fear that he might end up in prison, and that very fear drove her to treat her son harshly. She called him a "Meanie" and frankly threatened him: "Brad, you're gonna end up like Uncle Tony—in jail!" Without realizing it, her powerful words became abuse that was goading her only son straight to prison.

Such negative predictions are frighteningly common. They are made with the belief and hope that children will be motivated to avoid such disasters, and once in a while that happens. Far more commonly than one likes to imagine, however, these predictions become curses that sound doom to a child's ears. Children who receive this kind of abuse come to believe they will be the sort of creature their parents predict.

For a number of years I worked in a home for unmarried

mothers. As I probed each young woman's history, I un-earthed a significant truth. An energetic, beautiful girl would begin to assert her independence. Frightened parents saw her as becoming rebellious and wayward. They would increase restrictions only to see her kick even harder against them.

Eventually, in panic and despair, a father (commonly) would pronounce, "Eileen, you're just going to be a prostitute! A whore is what you will become!" This particular victim of such verbal abuse stated clearly, "My father told me so many times I'd be a whore that I decided I'd be one. He gave me the name and I began to play the game! So here I am!" Fortunately, with intensive help, Eileen was restored to a really fine life, but at an immense cost!

Sometimes the mother dishes out more of the abuse on daughters. "Dawn, you'll be the death of me one day!" her mother scolded. Dawn was a mischievous girl, constantly creating chaos through her escapades. Because they loved her, her parents had to repeatedly correct her. Her mother was burdened with most of the discipline, and she understandably wearied of it!

Dawn at first suffered twinges of remorse every time her mother mentioned being the death of her. But over time it became just another empty saying that lost its impact—as had the rest of her parents' words. She just refused to curb her adventurous spirit and continued getting into difficulty.

She was only twelve when Dawn overheard her parents' earnest discussions and noticed their anxious faces. One day the unbearable truth was revealed. Dawn's mother had cancer. She was soon in the hospital for lengthy periods and simply could not get the housework done any longer. Night after night, Dawn cried herself to sleep. Her dear mother was going to die. And it was all her fault. Hadn't her mother told her so repeatedly?

No words of reassurance could comfort the girl's broken heart. Plagued by deep guilt, Dawn began to punish herself in an effort to relieve the unbearable pain of believing she was responsibile for her mother's illness and impending death.

What Dawn and Brad experienced is typical of a special sort of verbal abuse. Parents all want their children to behave properly, study hard, and be responsible. But verbally abusive parents attempt to achieve these goals through unwittingly making them feel guilty. Brad's parents forecast a gloomy future for him—life in prison. And Dawn's mother tried to motivate her to behave better by predicting that her antics would actually kill her!

Neither set of parents ever imagined their dire prophecies would be fulfilled. Neither did Eileen's parents believe their proclamation of her immorality actually helped push her into a promiscuous life style. But we know such "curses" do have a profound impact on the lives of children—and usually, in a negative manner.

WITHHOLDING APPROVAL

Faith proudly carried home her report card from her first semester in junior high. It had been a frightening and difficult transition. Gone was the security of sixth grade where she was successful and knew everyone. Now Faith had to find her way from class to class every hour and even squeeze in time to visit her locker. Having so many different teachers was all new and she had gotten to know only a few of her fellow students.

With conscientious diligence, this pre-teen girl had learned to adapt to her teachers, figured out how to get to her classes on time, and studied hard. Her first report card was a source of personal pride: all A's, except for one B in math. This school used an entirely new system for teaching math that Faith had yet to master. But certainly, she had tried hard and was pleased with her own progress!

Tentatively, Faith handed her report card to her dad. Without any comment regarding the five A's, he asked, "Why did you get that B? How did Cindy do? Surely you can do as well as she can!" Struggling to hide her anxious tears, Faith tried to explain her difficulties as well as her efforts. Her father, however, was unmoved. He demanded sternly that she work harder and bring up that grade. His daughter must be the best!

Few fathers recognize how immeasurably important their approval is to their children. At each age and stage of life, everyone yearns intensely for a father's approval and his expression of pride in their achievements.

Abuse in this case was actual as well as symbolic. Faith's father failed to take pride in her efforts and the top-notch grades she did make, thereby robbing her of an important source of self-esteem. Her father's unfavorable comparison with her classmate catapulted her into grief. Not only did he steal her well-deserved pride in such hard work, he laid upon her the heavy demand to somehow be perfect—on top of the heap!

DAMAGING LABELS

Elaine was overjoyed at being a mother. Her first-born son was a fine and delightful baby. The new grandmother had come to visit for a few days to help until her daughter regained her strength. Their time together offered opportunities to leisurely reminisce about Elaine's own childhood and anticipate her brand new role as a mom.

Grandmother was startled during such a talk to hear Elaine say, "Mother, there's one thing I will never say about my son! I will never let anyone think he is shy. When I was little, I used to stick to you like glue whenever strangers were visiting. I just felt safer at your side. But you would tell them I was your 'shy child.' I hated that, but the more you said it, the more I actually felt insecure and became shy!"

Grandmother's eyes filled with tears as she realized what she had so unwittingly done in labeling her child. She was anxious to interpret her old feelings and actions to her adult child and find forgiveness. Elaine's mother wanted people to admire and love her child. She was afraid they might see the young girl as snobbish or rude, and felt their frequent visitors could accept shyness more comfortably.

Elaine's mother really believed that she was doing her child a favor by interpreting her reserved disposition as shyness. So immersed in caring about what others thought, she neglected to observe the hurts she inflicted on her own child. Somewhat later, Elaine's mother had discovered that it didn't matter very much what others thought about her or her children, but some damage had already been done. Avoid labeling your children!

Abuse is often unintentional and unrecognized; therefore, forgiveness is never sought and healing is difficult to find. It's quite normal to want others to love your children. Just be careful that you do not try too hard to make that happen. Check out any descriptive term you give your child. Is it one you yourself would be proud to wear? Is it a word your child may experience as belittling and hurtful? Verbal abuse is surprisingly easy to administer, even with the best of intentions!

SILENT SCREAMS

For the "umpteenth" time that evening, Jane reminded her ten-year-old son to do his homework. Yet Kent dawdled and refused to get busy. At last she had had it! Instead of a tirade, Jane simply *looked* at her son. The frustration and concern she felt blazed in her eyes and burned into his heart. "Mom," Kent pleaded, "quit yelling at me!"

Actually, his mother had not uttered a single angry word

at this point. But her look was indeed screaming her feelings. Most verbal abuse is spoken aloud. But body language alone can express more intense anger than one might intend. And that anger, with its implied rejection or disapproval, can hurt dreadfully.

Perhaps you can recall similar experiences. Can you picture the face of your father or mother as they corrected you? Did you ever see the intense anger or disgust that made you shrink? If you had difficulty looking directly into their eyes, it is quite likely you were afraid of their silent screams. One patient of mine had such parents. She described herself as feeling like "a tiny speck on a big apple." Her parents' wrath had literally caused her ego to shrivel.

We'll discuss later how to prevent and remedy the abuse body language or words inflict on children. It is of the utmost importance, however, that you develop a sensitivity to your child—about what you say, how you speak, and how you look. As you observe your child's facial expression, be aware of your own inner feelings. Whenever possible, avoid frowns of anger, worried looks, or strong disapproval. Granted, there are times when such expressions are both right and necessary for effective correction. But they should be the exception, not the rule!

✦ ✦ ✦

Study Questions

1. Describe incidents when you overheard your parents hurling abusive words at each other. In what ways has such emotional damage shaped your own sexual identity?

2. If married, in what ways do you feel your own marital adjustment has been handicapped or hampered by childhood verbal abuse?

3. Describe specific childhood incidents when your parents yelled at you about negative traits. How did this make you feel? What did you do with those feelings? Do you experience similar emotions now?

4. In what ways did your parents nag you or demand perfection? Describe times when your parents would withhold approval if you failed to measure up to their standards.

5. List any abusive names or damaging labels your parents may have called you and describe any negative impact such "curses" may have had on your life.

6. Were you ever compared with another family member in a negative way (e.g., "You're going to turn out just like your Uncle Tony!") and has that prediction been fulfilled in any way? If so, describe how.

FOUR

Sibling Rivalry
Gone Awry

✦ ✦ ✦

THE VITAL IMPORTANCE OF A FAMILY'S climate or atmosphere is almost impossible to overemphasize. It influences the degree of safety family members experience and delineates the total network of complex relationships that form, grow, and change with time.

While that climate is initiated by the parents, their children quickly sense it and build upon it. Darlene, the third of five children, illustrates this fact clearly. From birth, she and her mother were always at odds. She was not the magazine-cover beautiful baby that her mother had wanted. She cried loudly—and always, so it seemed, just as her mother was trying to catch a nap.

As Darlene grew, her mother believed her to be a demanding and even tyrannical child. Whenever there was a fight or something was broken, Darlene got the blame. Mother accused her of being clumsy, careless, selfish, worthless, and mean. She predicted that Darlene would drive her crazy.

The other children quickly caught on to this strategy. Her

brothers and sisters learned how to siderail their own misconduct on Darlene. They, too, began to blame her for everything bad that happened. When their mother seemed to readily accept their reports, this game paid rich dividends for each of them. Darlene inexorably followed the trail that ended in her being the family scapegoat.

Most of you know that a scapegoat is a creature that bears the sins of others, shouldering the blame and responsibility for their wrongdoing. Such a situation is all too common in families. It results in a climate of confusion, dishonesty, and guilt—and for the lonely scapegoat, fear, worthlessness, and hopelessness.

From birth, Darlene received so many curses from her family that she came to believe she was a bad child. Since her best efforts to be good were totally discounted, she soon learned to play her role and behave badly wherever she was. Acting naughty took less effort and often was more fun anyway. But she also learned to punish herself for such badness. Her body became a scarred monument to the verbal abuse that penetrated all of her life.

Perhaps you have also suffered such verbal abuse from both your parents and your siblings. Please try to believe that you were not and are not "bad." Such parents almost always misunderstand that particular child. They may see in the youngster traits of someone who offended them long ago. They have usually forgotten the time and the person, but they cannot forget the feelings that belong to their past. If the person reminds them of such an offense, they at last find excuses for getting even. The child can become not only the scapegoat victim of his or her own childhood but of the parents' as well.

As you learn more about your family history, you may discover that you truly were not the culprit. Such information needs to find a way to penetrate not only your mind but also your heart. When you know the truth about your scapegoat role, you can free yourself from the false guilt and perceived worthlessness you have endured.

NEGATIVE POWER

Let's look at another example of child-to-child verbal abuse. This true story was not influenced by parents, but shows how one child can learn to exercise negative power over another.

"You're the laziest person I ever knew!" Kirk was out of breath and shaking with anger. He was hot and tired from raking the huge lawn of thick grass all by himself. His sister was confined to bed, sick with the aftermath of another bout with strep throat. Jill felt sicker than she looked, and the doctor had ordered her to stay in bed.

She tried to explain her illness to her older brother, pleading for understanding. Jill loved and admired her tall teen-aged brother and did not know how to respond to his rage. But Kirk was not listening to her. After even more vehement statements about her irresponsibility and his hard work, the exhausted youth stalked out of her room.

Jill lay helpless and devastated. Could it be, she wondered, that the doctor was wrong? Perhaps she *should* get up and help. Maybe she *was* lazy. She did love to read and one of her joys in life was to lie on the grass watching the fleecy white clouds change shapes. Yes, probably she was lazy. Jill decided that day that as soon as she was well, she would be the hardest worker in the family. Never again could Kirk call her lazy.

In fact, Jill grew to be a workaholic. From early in the morning until late at night she learned to fill her days with activities. This example reveals a very significant fact about the power of words to hurt. The most destructive impact of verbal abuse comes from the fact that the words contain a modicum of truth. Jill could see that her dreamer personality did appear to be lazy. Her parents often lectured her because she read so avidly that she sometimes forgot her duties. She could readily see her brother's exhaustion and understand his need for help.

The power of words to hurt also lies in the degree of significance their victim assigns to the perpetrator. Jill loved and admired her older brother. She loved to play games with him and recognized his finer side that usually controlled his capacity for cruelty.

Once again, those crucial, cruel words were life-shaping. Jill made a decision that lasted a lifetime because of Kirk's tirade—or at least partially due to him. Perhaps you also had a brother or sister who verbally abused you. Like many people, you may even avoid seeing family members because you feel tense, anxious, or even frightened around them.

Let's examine Jill's situation more closely as it was processed through later counseling. These further insights may help to free you from your fears and heal your old hurts. You may even find the courage to explore a whole new relationship as an adult.

1. Kirk was much older than his sister. Jill had attributed to her brother something of a hero status, giving him vast power over her emotions. This kept her from being aware of Kirk's own insecurities that had prompted his tirade. Actually her brother had been ill a great deal when he was young and perhaps he himself had felt lazy or inadequate. To accuse someone else of those faults undoubtedly gave Kirk a sorely needed sense of power—not a healthy one, to be sure, but the best he could find then.

2. Once Jill could understand with her adult mind this episode so vividly recalled from her childhood, she could deal with it. The information she gleaned helped

her understand her brother's cruel words and enabled her to forgive him.

3. Jill began to see herself in a more positive light, no longer the helpless girl she once was. She found an opportunity to discuss this incident with Kirk and a few others as well. To her joy, Jill discovered that he was ashamed of his old behaviors. In fact, he was still so insecure that he had never gotten up the courage to tell her how sorry he was. Great warmth grew between the brother and sister because this victim would not settle for separation and pain.

4. Another benefit for Jill was the discovery that her brother had been wrong. She was not lazy at all! Much of her life had been expended in over-working to prove to herself—and unconsciously, to Kirk—that she was really worthwhile and industrious. She could now establish a better balance in work, play, and rest then she had ever known.

Like Darlene, Phyllis had been the scapegoat of her entire family. Actually, she was by far the most capable of the children. When her growing successes began to reveal their own deficiencies, her brothers and sisters ganged up on her and labeled her "stupid" and "awkward." They laughed at her and excluded her from their activities.

In an attempt to prove her siblings wrong and demonstrate her capabilities, Phyllis studied harder and gained a graduate degree. She practiced dancing and music to acquire grace and coordination. But each time she discussed her new successes, she received only put-downs from her family. They accused her of being a snob, too good for them. You can imagine her anguish when all of her efforts proved futile. Phyllis could not gain the coveted pride and approval of those she so desperately loved and whose approval she craved.

It was only through professional help that this young woman found peace. Her counselor enabled her to perceive many important truths about her situation.

1. Her family would never be able to accept her or be proud of her. This was certainly a cause for grieving, but Phyllis could understand this process and eventually recover from her grief.
2. The family's treatment of her had little to do with Phyllis herself, except as it reflected her excellent achievements. Their rejection clearly came from their own inability to compete and their immense jealousy of her talents.
3. Phyllis need not allow their pettiness to spoil either her success or her own enjoyment of it. She had the power and the permission to be her own person—to thrill at the vast challenges of the life she herself had worked so hard to attain.

Reconciliation is sometimes impossible. The loss of that natural wish and dream is grievous. But once the grief is past, exciting new vistas can be found. Without enduring this process, however, the old unconscious habits of trying once more to merit the pleasure of one's family will mar or even destroy those adventures into a new world.

JEALOUSY AND RESENTMENT

"Mama's pet! Mama's pet!" Melvin chanted to his sister. They had been playing a game of checkers and Karen had won. Melvin hated to lose, so he had stomped off refusing to play anymore. When her brother refused to continue the game she was enjoying, Karen went to their mother seeking help.

Their mother was understandably concerned over Melvin's poor sportsmanship. She lectured him about that fault and demanded they play just one more game. Melvin felt he had not been understood and spat out his hurt and resentment toward both Mom and Karen in his angry words.

Sibling rivalry is a universal situation in families with more than one child. Much of it is healthy and motivates children in a type of competition that is most often energizing. Such positive motivation should be encouraged. However, when the rivalry stems from perceived parental favoritism, it usually becomes highly destructive.

In ancient times, Cain saw his brother Abel's sacrifice as more acceptable to God. And so he killed his brother. From then until now, seeing a sibling favored above oneself prompts pain, jealousy, and often rage. The hurt stems from the implication that one's own worth is not as great as the other's.

Mark was playing outside in the garden, building a smooth road with deep ditches out of freshly dug flower beds. It was a warm spring day; the world was full of warmth and the promise of a fine, free summer. As Mark was deeply concentrating on his intricate road building, he inadvertently overheard a conversation between his mother and her friend. From the window above him, these words drifted out and immediately clouded over not only the beautiful spring day but the rest of Mark's life as well.

"I shouldn't say this," his mother was stating, "but Carl is such a great son. I'd have to say that he's just my favorite child."

Those words deeply wounded Mark's spirit and caused him to resent his only brother. He vowed that he would show Mom who was the best. Mark became a strong, hard-working, highly respected man. But he could not unload the pain and resentment he felt toward Carl. His mother's powerful words—however innocently spoken—had done their work. The two brothers lived out their adult lives with bitterness in their hearts. As they competed for proof of their intrinsic worth, they unconsciously kept the childhood struggle alive.

Even though many times unintended, verbal abuse can carry the same tragic results. Mark's mother loved him very much, but it was apparent that Carl had won her special favor. He seemed to intuitively know how to please her. The truth is that Carl resembled his uncle—the brother who was especially dear to his mother. Nevertheless, Mark had been verbally abused. Those words wrought deep emotional pain that created scars, influenced his self worth, and produced cruel jealousy and resentment toward his only brother.

Sometimes sibling rivalry springs from another source. Kitty was one of those rare lovely girls who seemed to be good at everything. She won the academic competitions, the athletic events, and the good citizenship awards as well. She was attractive and knew just what colors and styles made her look the best. Her older sister simply could not measure up to Kitty's successes. Gretchen looked for every defect in her younger sister.

One time she cruelly commented to her sister, "Linda thinks you're stuck up. You think she's your best friend, but that's not what she told me!"

What abusive words! Jealous of Kitty's giftedness, Gretchen felt that she had to cut her sister down in some way. She was able to find that inevitable spot of vulnerability and stab into it the poison of her own pain—using Kitty's best friend as the dagger.

Often children themselves see their siblings as outstripping them in various ways. They make their own unfavorable comparisons. Instead of feeling happy over their own successes, these unhappy kids attempt to tear down their siblings who overshadow them in some way. In this manner they try to narrow the gap between their perceived inferiority and their sibling's success.

Parents need to understand the basis for unhealthy sibling rivalry. It may be due to their own partiality, as in the case of Mark. It may emanate from a child's own perception of his or her unworthiness. Or it may stem from a resemblance a child has to a problem relative, as in the case of Brad.

Whatever the cause, one basic dynamic underlies all destructive sibling rivalry. The bottom line boils down to this: *"I'm not as good as she/he is—not worth as much!"* The following tactics may be helpful in overcoming such damaging feelings.

1. Review your family relationships. Was verbal abuse from your siblings related to your parents' preferences? Did they learn to treat you as a scapegoat in the same way your parents did?

2. To avoid blaming your past, look promptly at your parents' childhood. Did they suffer similar abuse through their siblings and parents? And do you perhaps in some way remind them of their abusers? In this area, try to understand their hurts are now scars so deep that they may have forgotten the original wounds. They merely act out those feelings impulsively, without consciously understanding why!

3. Do you recognize jealousy in your siblings that explains their cruel words? Like Phyllis, it may be that the more you have worked at success to gain their approval, the more inferior they have felt. Being unable to tolerate such feelings—and being totally unsuccessful at competing with you—they may have tried to tear you down to their own level.

4. Understanding the reasons for abuse by your brothers or sisters does not excuse them. But such insight can set you free from guilt and any sense of inadequacy you may have felt. And it can enable you to truly forgive them. We'll discuss this later in more detail in Chapter 17.

Your increased awareness of these family dynamics will help you to treat your adult siblings in a more kindly, comfortable manner. In time, you may find a gradual change in your estranged relationships with them. As you master these skills, you will hopefully alleviate the annoyance of sibling fights, even as adults. Furthermore, you will help to prevent the development in your own children of much of the verbal abuse between brothers and sisters. A more harmonious and enjoyable family is well worth the effort required.

❖ ❖ ❖

Study Questions

1. Describe any childhood incidents when you were verbally abused by your siblings. Even if you cannot remember specific times and people, how did such abuse make you feel?

2. Were you ever treated as the family scapegoat? If so, describe how. Are you able to now believe that you were not the actual culprit?

3. In what ways were you made to feel like you were a "bad" child? How did you learn to play a role accordingly?

4. What family members do you now avoid seeing because you feel tense, anxious, or frightened around them? Try to identify the reasons behind such feelings.

5. Describe any incidents when you were called abusive names, laughed at, ridiculed, rejected, or excluded by your siblings. How did this make you feel? Did you try harder to gain their approval as a consequence?

6. What sibling rivalry for your parents' love or approval did you experience? In what ways did your parents show any destructive favoritism that damaged your self-worth or unfavorably compare you with a sibling in a way that produced lasting feelings of inferiority?

FIVE

The Transgenerational Triangle

✦ ✦ ✦

TO HER UTTER DISMAY, Gini found herself screaming again! She felt so ashamed of herself—it seemed like the hundredth time today she had exploded in anger. Her two pre-schoolers were fairly normal children, full of energy and wanting to spend all of it today. Gini understood that, but when they slammed doors and ran through the house, her lamps and glasses trembled until she feared they would break.

"Why must you kids always be so wild? Why can't you ever quiet down? You're giving me a headache!" she shouted. Because they were accustomed to Gini's yelling, they ignored her until she reached the part about the headache. They really loved their mom and didn't want to give her a headache. They just enjoyed their own brand of yelling and intense activity. Why did Mom have to always yell about their good fun?

After even more very loud lecturing, Gini ordered the children outside. The silence of the next few minutes allowed the screaming of her own mother to echo in her mind. She had almost forgotten it, but the slam of the door made her remember her own avenue of escape as a child from the angry disapproval of her mom.

Gini began to wonder. Do all the mothers in this family yell? Her sister did and she suspected her grandmother had yelled at her mother. Maybe screaming was genetic. If so, perhaps she could never overcome it. She was haunted by the scared, sad faces of her children as they drew away from her angry words. How could her behavior so quickly transform them from carefree children who were excited at play, into angry, scared, sad, little urchins? What sort of witch had she become? Where was the ugly broom on which she traveled?

Gini left her painful reverie to go and call her own mother. She poured out her guilt and remorse to the mom she loved, and then asked, "Mom, where did you learn to yell at us?"

Silence hung on the other end of the line. Her mother was too stunned by Gini's question to respond immediately and almost reflexively started to deny that she had ever made a habit of yelling. But Gini's cry for help was too genuine and anguished to ignore or treat lightly. Her mother had almost forgotten, but when she stopped to think about her days as a young mother, she had to admit that she had often yelled at her children. And then her own memories flooded back, as her mind echoed not just her own screaming, but the harsh tones of her own mother as well.

At last, Gini's mother began to reminisce aloud. She told her grown daughter about her own childhood, so filled with harshness and fear. She explained how she had overcome that fear by learning to yell at her younger brother and her dolls. Screaming at them made her feel powerful and kept away the lurking fear that her mother might send her away as she had sometimes threatened.

Gini's mother could also recall visits from her grand-mother. In fact, she used to stay with her grandparents for many months at a time. Grandma would often speak sharply to her, as well as to her mother. The memory of her mother's face as her grandmother reprimanded her was as fresh as yesterday.

Gini finally understood how verbal abuse is learned. In order to survive it with even a shell of strength and some degree of personal worth, you had to master it yourself. The sad part of that process was its inevitably being passed on like a legacy to the next generation. Gini determined to break the chains of this horrible habit. And she did!

BREAKING THE CHAIN

Many of you can recall similar experiences from your own childhood, and some of you are even now carrying on the practice. You, like Gini, can be the one to break that chain. *By realizing what you are doing,* you have taken the first step, painful as it is.

The next step is equally tough: *you must believe you can change.* Verbal abuse is not welded into your physical make-up or brain, but purely a habit that must be broken. You must give yourself the permission to change.

Next, *develop a plan.* Few habits are broken instanta-neously. You must work at changing. Decide what you will say instead of abusive words. How will you gain mastery over the old emotions that propel you into the habit of verbal abuse? By recognizing them before they explode and re-placing them with kind and thoughtful statements, you can do just that.

Another part of your plan for change is the *inclusion of a helper.* All of us need a trusted friend—one who can be hon-est without being cruel, one who has your best interest at heart. When you have slipped back into old habits and feel you will never be able to change, call your friend. State clearly that you are discouraged and need some reinforcement. Before you call, think out precisely what kind of help you may need. Your friend will be able to help you much more effectively if you can clarify how that may best be accomplished. Just don't be afraid to ask.

One of the most successful forms of disciplining small children is the use of *"time out."* Borrowed from our sports world, time out is space for reviewing bad plays or mistakes, time to plan for an especially important play, or time to rest before resuming the game. A tired, verbally abusive mother once taught me that Moms and Dads, too, need time out.

If you really want to break the generations-long chain of verbal abuse, give yourself a break whenever you feel you are losing control of your emotions. Slip away from whatever or whoever is pushing you to your breaking point. The only place for privacy may be the bathroom! Wherever you can find seclusion, take advantage of it. Get quiet. Think. Decide how you want to act and speak. Even rehearse your words, if you will. Then go back and face the stressful situation, calmly and lovingly. The entire atmosphere around you will begin to be transformed as you master this new technique of taking time out.

Prayer is especially helpful at this point. God wants to help you in these kinds of everyday trials of life. Ask him to give you the necessary love and wisdom to deal with the stressful demands of raising children. You may be surprised by the joy of discovering that he is there waiting to respond to your needs!

Finally, just be *tenacious*. Any habit is hard to break. Getting free from the practices that are interwoven with your past and your deepest emotions is immensely more difficult. You must stick with it. How many people have almost accomplished their goal, only to give up at the last ditch in the road. Don't give up!

SWEET AND MELLOW, OR GRUFF AND GROUCHY?

As we grow older, we are just what we were when we were young—only more so! I read this concept long ago, and review it with some anxiety as I have grown older. I ask myself, have I sweetened and mellowed with increased age? Or am I more pessimistic and grouchy?

Carey was only four when she endured the unintentional verbal abuse of her grandmother. She and her family were visiting her grandparents with her new baby brother. Carey's mixed feelings of pride and displacement were confusing to her. Still a little uncertain in her role as big sister, she felt particularly vulnerable.

When dinnertime came, Grandma began to arrange the seating around the big oak table. Realizing Carey's height would make it impossible for her to sit on an ordinary chair, Grandma searched for a "booster." She asked the little girl if a telephone directory would lift her high enough to eat comfortably. Carey agreed politely.

The visiting family lived in a big city with a very thick directory, but Grandma lived in a village of only a few hundred. She laughingly brought out the little booklet that served the local telephone customers and placed it on Carey's chair. The little girl, not wanting to be rude, looked in amazement at her grandmother's apparent solution to her need for a boost at the dining table and fell silent. Her face must have expressed both the shock and confusion she felt. What most pained her and left emotional scars for three decades to come was Grandma's laughter.

Of course children sometimes have funny reactions to a variety of situations. But what her grandmother had intended as an innocent joke seemed to the child like ridicule. Grandma went on to find an adequate booster for Carey's chair, but this sensitive little child never again really trusted Grandma. Carey locked away the injustice of her grandmother's unexpected treatment until she became an adult.

In fact, only when her own child suffered taunting on one occasion was the memory of her pain triggered. Discussing it finally relieved much of the built-up hurt she had endured for so long.

Abuse in all of its forms passes on from one generation to the next. It is almost certain that Carey's grandmother had experienced verbal abuse expressed through ridicule. In fact, she grew up in a family whose primary humor was just that. Since Grandma enjoyed a hearty laugh, she had learned to perpetrate that practice. And Carey was an available target.

Children are so vulnerable—bundles of receptor nerves that see, listen to, and sense everything about them. Their concrete thought processes are often not capable of sorting out when a joke is just funny or when it actually pokes ridicule at them.

Carey's story may remind you of the piercing pain of having some family member make fun of you. No abuse is ever justified! At your very worst, you did not merit abuse from your parents or grandparents, nor your brothers or sisters. Such treatment stems from insensitivity, old habits that need changing, or personal insecurities that seek relief by tearing down another. Hear this clearly—you were not bad, stupid, or unworthy!

Claude and Dan, age twelve and thirteen, loved to visit on their grandfather's farm. In the summertime, their parents would transport the boys and their bicycles to the country and leave them for several days. The brothers loved even the hard work of helping their aging grandfather with baling hay and milking the cows.

Only recently, Dan reminisced about those days now some five decades past. The dour face of his grandmother was as clear in his memory as if it were last week. Her words were irritable at best, and often he felt she was truly caustic. The poison of her complaints and critical comments was bitter even in his memories, himself now the "older man" just as his grandfather had been.

Dan recalls riding his bicycle to a nearby village with Claude. The country roads were smooth with very little traffic, and the village small and friendly. Riding to town for a strawberry ice cream cone was a safe and happy adventure for the two young boys. But the luscious taste of strawberry ice cream is still bitter to Dan because of his grandmother's sharp words.

Upon their return, she had grouched, "You boys shouldn't have gone into town. You could've been hit by a car. You made me worry all the time you were gone." Yet she herself had given them permission to go, reluctantly of course. Certainly, her worry demonstrated her concern for the welfare of those boys. But her unloving, angry expression of that caring had twisted her genuine caring into a toxin that poisoned an otherwise marvelous memory, even for a now older adult. Protection of children can be done gently and must be balanced with common sense that permits safe exploring and memorable adventures.

Dan and Claude were not bad boys and had done nothing wrong. They had sought permission, ridden their bikes, eaten their ice cream cones, and returned home safely. Their grandmother failed to acknowledge their capabilities. She wrongly put them in the dilemma of allowing them to go and then criticizing them for doing so!

If you yourself suffered from this kind of abuse, my hope is that you can see yourself in as clear and kindly a light as you perceive Dan and Claude. So much of the recovery from the scars of verbal abuse depends upon recognizing your innocence and seeing the error in your abuser.

UNINTENTIONAL BARBS

Sometimes grandparents can be verbally cruel without realizing it. Gruff Grandfather Neil had a chance to see his first grandchild when she was only six months old. After a tiring trip, the new parents were exhausted but excited to show off their beautiful new baby. With the comfort of her pacifier, Nancy had fallen asleep at last.

After Grandfather Neil had glanced only briefly at the infant, he grabbed the pacifier, threw it to the end of the bassinet, and stated tersely, "She doesn't need that!" Nancy's mother was at first shocked into silence. She hurried to the kitchen to weep her tears of pain and rage alone. Her father's comment was not what she had expected, but was instead a painful reminder of all her years growing up.

Dad had always been critical, rarely complimentary, and so powerful in his harshness. She had hoped a new baby might elicit some hidden warmth and gentleness. The desired change in behavior failed to happen—as so often is the case. Old habits are hard to break. Verbal abuse can become habitual.

Nancy did use that unhappy experience to learn some essential facts. She clearly understood that her father's perpetually critical attitude toward her was unwarranted. He was simply a strongly opinionated man, always right in his mind, and powerfully blunt in stating his judgments and verdicts. Pained as she was at this greeting of her new baby, Nancy was finally able to free herself from her childhood pattern of vainly trying to merit her father's approval. It was he who was incapable of giving it. He had taken on as his role condemnation and criticism, no matter how abusive that was.

By contrast, John doted on his grandchildren. When his own children were little, he had been a workaholic within a large corporation. Those irreplaceable years whizzed by like the speedometer on his well-used car. At his retirement, John suddenly realized that his own children were strangers. He had almost no memories of them, and even the family photos were of little help in recreating the missing years. He could vaguely recollect disciplinary actions his wife had prompted. With greater effort he could even recall some pretty harsh statements he had made in an attempt to correct and motivate his kids.

Now John had time to spare and enjoyed these visits with his precious grandchildren. They lived nearby so he was even able to see them regularly. But the critical nature that had made John so good in his job was still focused on his own children. When an attitude or a behavior in the youngest generation became apparent, John inevitably found an opportunity to inform his children—for their own good, of course.

"You're far too hard on your daughter," he told his daughter. "You need to give her some space. She's only ten. You expect too much of her. You should quit working and be around your children. They need you!"

John's daughter, of course, reacted with the intense anger that only pain can create. How dare *he* criticize her parenting! He certainly had never been there when she needed him. And now here he was siding with her children against her. It certainly wasn't fair. But he was still her father and she felt she couldn't say to him all the hurting, angry words that raced through her mind. So the old estrangement grew even stronger and she avoided him as much as possible.

Even though John meant well, his words to his daughter were abusive through the obvious pain they conveyed. By definition, abuse is *any action or communication that inflicts the needless pain of condemnation and leaves lifelong scars.* John's earlier parenting involvement had been minimal. The significant encounters he did have with his children were times of punishment, and he had failed to build the set of happy, loving interactions with which to balance those disciplinary actions. In his own heart, John's intentions were to enjoy with his children's children those special times he had missed. Good intentions, however, are not enough.

Almost certainly many of you identify all too closely with

John's adult daughter. The anger that desperately wants to retaliate may seem a familiar response. If you give in to that desire, the very real danger is that you could become just like the abuser! Trying to understand is much more fruitful, and likely to change the relationship for the better.

Sadly, John could not go back and rework his own children's early years, but he vaguely knew he had been wrong. He sincerely wanted his daughter to be a better parent than he himself had been. If you can understand this motive, perhaps you can forgive the faulty methods grandparents sometimes use. And perhaps you can even believe that they deeply love you and that their mistakes were their own—rather than having anything to do with your unworthiness!

A WORD TO WELL-MEANING GRANDPARENTS

Let me close this chapter with a word to well-meaning grandparents. Most young parents need considerable help in teaching and raising their children and they usually welcome positive suggestions. So let me suggest some ways in which your desire to help can become more effectiveness.

1. First of all, take a long look back. How did you relate with your own children? Don't be either too critical or too easy on yourself, but look honestly at those years.
2. When you clearly see your mistakes, find a way to verbally make amends. Take your children to lunch and talk. Or else write a letter or make a phone call. Tell them of your new understanding about the old wounds you inflicted. Let your children know how sorry you are for *your* mistakes. You may explain why you did those painful things. Above all, ask for forgiveness and seek their help in making changes even now.
3. Once healing of the old wounds is progressing well, you may be able to further strengthen the relationships. Ask your adult children if they would like to

spend some time sharing some of the wisdom you have gleaned over the years. I find all grandparents have a wealth of wisdom but often fail to recognize or value it, or fail to focus it clearly so its enlightening glow is wasted. Don't let that happen to you.

4. If you can develop a more loving relationship with your own children—and with effort and patience you can—you will be ready to teach them. To be effective, that teaching must be positive and constructive. Start with what you see your children doing *right.* It is especially helpful if you see them doing some things even better than you did. Describe their strengths and specifically state what you most admire about their parenting.

5. Finally, where your children's inevitable mistakes must become your focus, be gentle. Try to find a connection between their mistakes and your own. By describing your errors and reminding your children of the pain these behaviors inflicted, you can help them to feel the same pain with your grandchildren. Such empathy can be a strong motivator in attempting to change poor habits. You are next able to say, "If I could do it over, here's how I'd do it." How could any adult child reject such gentle, loving wisdom?

As you can clearly see, this is a lengthy process which requires dedicated time and effort. Its success depends on your sensitivity to your children, absolute honesty, and careful selection of loving and encouraging words. You may even have to learn an entirely new vocabulary! How easy it is to blurt out, "You're making such a terrible mistake!" "Here's what I did wrong" conveys the same message, but in a palatable form.

You can become a champion grandparent by helping to heal the hurts you unwittingly inflicted on your children. You can help stop verbal abuse from moving on into yet another generation!

✦ ✦ ✦

Study Questions

1. List any abusive habits that you learned from your parents' behavior. How do you think these same patterns were rooted in their own upbringing? How could you raise this issue with your parents or grandparents in a non-threatening way in order to improve mutual understanding?

2. What kind of plan can you develop to help you work at changing your own abusive habits? What will you say instead of hurtful words when you feel those old emotions rising within you?

3. What trusted friend can encourage and support you in your efforts to overcome abusive habits? List specific ways in which they could be of help. Call your friend and seek his/her willingness to help you.

4. Have you ever used the "time out" approach when you are losing emotional control? If yes, describe the results.

5. What incidents of intentional or unintentional verbal abuse from your grandparents can you recall?

6. In what ways are your parents now overly doting with your children or critical of you as a parent?

7. What changes would you like to see in your communication and relationship with your parents?

Part Two

Verbal Abuse outside the Family

SIX

Academic Stress

✦ ✦ ✦

FOR MORE THAN FIFTEEN YEARS, I have worked regularly as a consultant in various private and public schools. On the whole, the teachers, counselors, and administrators I have come to know so well are dedicated folks. All of these professionals frequently describe the verbal abuse aimed at them by rebellious students.

The names and labels applied to them are of the most vulgar type. Even more common are variations of the defiant statement, "You can't make me do anything I don't want to do." From kindergarten through senior year, many students test the mettle of any adult who represents authority. A teacher of over twenty years of experience recently reflected that rudeness has increased exponentially in the past several years.

After a ladies' luncheon where I was the speaker, a woman waited for some time to talk with me. She told me that as a teacher, she was especially committed to helping students find their special areas of interest and success. She viewed the field of education as a wonderful opportunity not only to educate minds but also to challenge young people to do something productive with their lives.

"But," she mourned, "I'm about to give up! So many of my students are indifferent and rude. And I can handle that, but I cannot stand the real abuse many others hand out." She went on to describe the curses, insults, and other forms of abuse she experienced at their hands. Many other teachers, mostly women, have shared similar concerns. This situation is deserving of some exploration.

Whenever I have had the opportunity, I have investigated the backgrounds of such abusive students. I have discovered that their mothers had usually suffered abuse as youngsters. These struggling women were so accustomed to taking verbal abuse that they unwittingly had allowed their children to abuse them. They heroically refused to abuse their children. But in avoiding inflicting the abuse they had suffered from their parents, these women had become permissive mothers—allowing their own children to get away with terrible abuse. The verbal abuse dished out at school was only a habit these young people had transferred from home.

Verbal abuse can evidence itself in many ways and for various reasons. If you are one of those mothers or teachers, it would be particularly helpful if you would team up with one another. Mothers, if you have tolerated verbal abuse from your children, be assured that you can correct that. But you are likely to need help. You teachers who have taken verbal abuse from your students, you too can help correct their abusiveness.

Mothers do not deserve abuse from their own children any more than they did from their parents. A loving mom recently sobbed out the story of her daughter. She had grown up deeply hurt by her parents' constant verbal tirades. So Harriet had determined to do exactly the opposite with her own offspring. At no point could she bring herself to correct her child's violently explosive outbursts. Now nearing middle-age, Harriet is enduring abuse from her pre-adolescent child almost as severe as her parents had administered.

Here are some suggestions for correcting abuse from students.

1. Meet and discuss the problem with the parents. It may take some extra time and energy, but you are expending those precious commodities anyway. Call the parents, write them, or if possible visit them at home. Certainly this direct approach is not always wise or possible, but is the best means to effective communication.
2. Share with the parents any positive information you can and make clear the child's potential. Without blame or accusation, discuss your concerns about the child's abusive patterns. Ask if the parents also have some concerns about this tendency.
3. Be prepared with a practical, easy-to-enforce plan for changing bad behavior—such as a reward for controlling such habits and a loss of some privileges for failing to correct them. The best rewards are the parents' own pride and pleasure in the child's efforts, coupled with extra time together in a pleasureable activity. The best punishment is the clear expression of the parents' displeasure, backed up by their willingness to carry out "grounding" from TV, telephone, and play for a specified time.

   If parents will follow through with such consequences, your major task as a teacher is to communicate consistently with them. Be careful, of course, not to "tattle." Keep a positive attitude and let the child know that both you and the parents are out for his or her good. The truth is that you care enough to stop the abusive talk—whether the angry words are directed at you, a peer, or the child's family.

4. Be sure you follow through by talking regularly with both the child and the parents. Emphasize the positive changes even more than the failures, but do not let a child get by with breaking the rules for better, loving communication. You *can* make a difference!

THE GAME OF DISTRACTION

For several years I enjoyed a guest lectureship in an education class at a nearby university. On one occasion, three students entered the large amphitheater late. Having made their way up to seats near the top where they were highly visible, these girls never stopped chatting and giggling. I tried to continue working with the remaining interested and involved students, but the disturbance was so great that it made an effective class impossible.

At last, I courteously commented that the talking was interfering with the lecture and discussion and asked if everyone would please be considerate. Almost predictably, those three students talked and giggled even more loudly. As I made an effort to block out the insulting behavior and enjoy the serious students for the rest of the hour, the class continued as well as we could.

Such distracting behavior can readily be classified as verbal abuse by these points:

1. They inflict pain on the teacher by their clear though unverbalized statement, "You are not worth listening to or respecting. I care nothing about you or your hard work, nor do I care about the other students."
2. Other teachers with whom I have talked find such distractions make them feel incapable of maintaining discipline or being otherwise effective in their profession. In many instances, such behavior can even influence them to change careers—a life-changing impact.

3. These teachers also say that the abuse they suffer from disorderly conduct in class tends to produce anger which they may displace on others. They find heroic effort is required to avoid becoming abusive themselves.

Similar but far more violent distractions are commonplace from elementary school on up. Even severe verbal abuse is often overlooked. Some schools attempt to exert their authority by suspending offending students. Commonly, parents themselves have long since given up, failing to exert any positive authority at home. With increasing frequency, I even find parents siding with rebellious, abusive children against the staff members.

GANGING UP ON THE TEACHER

Coreen had taught school for nearly twenty years. Eighth grade history was her favorite subject and she knew the material well. In fact, she knew it so well that the children in her classes had difficulty keeping up with her lectures. She was definitely a no-nonsense teacher and long ago had eliminated all jokes or humor. Coreen believed the students took advantage of such lightness and would not stick to their task of learning the facts of American history.

In recent years this dedicated teacher found her students less interested and much less willing to do homework and write papers. Very few seemed able to master the facts well enough to make top grades. The old camaraderie she once enjoyed with her students was now missing, and she even read a growing animosity in her students' attitudes.

One Monday morning as she was beginning class, most of the students suddenly stood up. At a prearranged signal, they picked up their chairs, turned them around, and sat with their backs to her desk—and to Coreen herself. They then opened their books, but ignored their teacher. All of this outrageous behavior was done without a word.

It is a paradox to think of verbal abuse without any spoken words. But the silent language of these rude young people was thundering its statement: "We don't like you! We won't respect you! And we won't even look at you!"

Only two angry youngsters had organized this action against Coreen. Yet these two were powerful enough to gain the cooperation of over twenty others. Coreen did not return to school for over a week. Gaining an apology from the guilty students demanded many hours of time from the principal and their parents. Though their silent abuse permanently scarred their teacher, the tough callouses created in their own hearts were even more tragic. If abuse is allowed to continue, the most serious damage it eventually accomplishes is in the heart of the perpetrator.

ABUSIVE TEACHERS

These examples of verbal and silent abuse by students could be repeated in countless variations. Whether abuse is the crude label of cursing, the rudeness of competing with teachers for control, or the silent retaliation of groups is irrelevant. The sad fact remains that a massive amount of verbal abuse as well as physical violence by our young people continues to wreak havoc in our schools.

I am increasingly troubled, however, by a growing number of teachers who also verbally abuse students. Of course this phenomenon is nothing new. One of my early school memories is of a teacher whose sarcasm was frequently aimed at me and my sister. This otherwise excellent teacher was commonly known for her sharp tongue.

On one occasion she made an unusually lengthy assignment, which happened to fall during a time when the chores on our farm were also unusually demanding. In a seldom used request for leniency, we explained the stress of our situation and asked for an extension of the deadline. Without any apparent consideration for our feelings, this woman yelled, "You poor girls! You must be the hardest working children in the whole county!"

My sister and I had no words nor experience with which to reply to her caustic words. Our shocked and frightened faces must have caused her to reconsider and grant us an extension. But her thoughtless words had already wounded our hearts and confused our minds.

Only recently I interviewed a fifteen-year-old boy who suffers from a learning disorder. School had become a painful experience of chronic defeat. Cliff had only one passion. He loved cars and auto mechanics and knew a great deal about these subjects. This teenager was overjoyed when one of his teachers focused the class on the value of airbags in cars, a marvelous safety device that can save many lives.

My young friend raised his hand timidly to comment about airbags. Cliff was excited that at long last, here was a subject he knew. His excitement, however, was short-lived. Could he have heard the teacher correctly? Unfortunately, he had. Her comment to the entire class was, "I said 'airbags,' Cliff, not 'air heads'!" His classmates all looked at him and roared their laughter. The teacher gloated—according to Cliff's description—at her witticism, while her embarrassed victim retreated in humiliation and rage.

In all likelihood, Cliff would soon think of a rude, abusive comment with which to get even with his teacher, who would then await her chance to retaliate. A tragically vicious cycle thus becomes established. Verbal abuse, like all forms of aggression, typically results in such a retaliatory interaction.

Frankie was only five, the youngest member of his kindergarten class. Perhaps he should have waited another year to start school, but he was bright, well-behaved, and seemed ready to go. But this small child had one habit which his teacher strongly disapproved; when Frankie was especially tired, or a bit bored, he would suck his thumb.

Lillian decided that she had just the cure for this babyish habit! One day she caught Frankie with his thumb in his mouth and quickly drew the attention of the entire class to him. When he immediately withdrew the offending thumb, Lillian insisted he replace it in his mouth. "Now, class," she stated, "this is an example of a baby. Isn't he cute?" Of course the children gleefully followed her example of laughing at this sweet, unsuspecting child. Without a physical touch but only the cruelty of her words, Lillian had stabbed the tender heart of a sensitive and loving child.

Such torment, even in today's narcissistic culture, is not frequent. But it does occur. If you are the parent of a young school child, be certain that you get to know his or her teacher well. Visit the class now and then if you suspect there is an unkind attitude. Be sure your child has not precipitated the teacher's abuse by some sort of hurtful misconduct. And then seek a conference to meet privately with the teacher. If necessary, visit with the principal to solicit help in stopping the verbal abuse of your child.

Peter's story was a bit different. This child had a habit of being exceptionally frank, almost to the point of rudeness. At times he could easily irritate a teacher with whom he had difficulty. Once offended, Peter had great trouble liking a teacher, and knowingly or not would begin to heckle such a person. One day, Peter made a comment in class that irritated his teacher. He realized he was wrong and remained silent until he had a legitimate question.

When he raised his hand, the teacher—not to be outdone by this impudent youth—sharply demanded, "Put your hand down!" Peter tried once more to raise his hand to ask for clarification of an assignment. Again the teacher yelled, "Peter, I said put your hand down!" This time he respectfully stated, "Please, I need to ask about the assignment." By this time, this poor woman was truly out of control. She threatened Peter with a trip to the principal's office and possible suspension from school.

No one won that battle of the wills. The teacher lost respect. Peter became even more angry to cover his fear and embarrassment. And he learned to keep his feelings and questions to himself. The scars of this teacher's humiliating words are still in his heart as an adult. He will never forget the year of her repeated verbal abuse.

It is possible for adults to allow themselves to react to children on their own level. When tempted to retaliate in kind, find the courage and wisdom to resist. Act like an adult, talk with clarity and firmness when those qualities are needed, but do not stoop to a child's behavior. How can she or he learn adult ways from an adult who reacts like a child?

Perhaps you can recall verbal abuse from a teacher. You may even have allowed the experience to limit your own academic achievements. If you can recall such a form of abuse, now is the time to unload your old hurt feelings and become free. Here are some steps to help you.

1. Find out any available information about that teacher. Your old classmates or another teacher or administrator may be able to help you, especially if you tell them why you need to know.
2. Use that information to reassure you that the abuse was caused by that person's problems, more than your stupidity or badness.
3. If you, like Peter, were by nature a mischievous questioner—perhaps even seen by your teacher as a heckler—simply forgive yourself and be sure you have overcome that habit. At least be sure that you no longer annoy others in such a manner.
4. Finally, explore your ambitions and dreams. If they have been lost because of some kind of abuse in the past, try to rediscover them. It's rarely too late to do so.

A dear friend of mind at the age of fifty-five is now in the process of earning a doctorate degree. Yet as a child, he suffered unbearable abuse by both his teachers and parents. You don't have to have a Ph.D. degree to recover from abuse, but by recovering you may yet achieve the goals you thought you had lost!

WHAT IF YOUR CHILD IS ABUSED IN SCHOOL?

In all likelihood, the current trend toward disrespect in schools will continue. Many of the efforts to improve the environment in our communities and educational systems seem to be ineffective. Academic achievement scores are falling and even our country's president is trying to secure laws that will restore educational excellence in our country.

In this time of national focus on education, parents must also take a serious look at the experience of their own children. The greatest opportunity for active change lies in correcting your children's own behavior. Even if they have an abusive teacher, help them learn to cope. Verbal abuse is part of life.

Millie is an example of this sad fact. During her fifth grade year, she discovered that school was not fun anymore. The warmth, fun, and good grades of the fourth grade classroom were all missing. Instead Millie went home almost daily with stories about some of her classmates being scolded and getting into trouble. She was rarely the victim of her teacher's harshness, but Millie began to live in dread of the day that could happen.

As her parents began to understand the situation, they debated their possible role in it. In order to support their child's teacher as much as possible, they had a talk with Millie. First of all, they encouraged her to understand that teachers were not all as superb as Miss Johnson, her fourth grade teacher. Furthermore, teachers are only people. Just like parents, they had good days and bad days and could be grouchy at times.

These wise parents suspected her teacher might be going through some difficult times and could really use Millie's support. They suggested ways in which she could offer it. She might explain to her friends, for example, some of the ideas her family had discussed and help them act more kindly toward this irritable lady. After all, this approach would make it easier on all of the students even if they didn't sincerely care how the teacher felt.

Slowly Millie's classmates began to follow her example. They all made it through that year and later learned that that year had, indeed, been difficult for the teacher. She had been in the midst of marital problems that terminated in a divorce. Years later that teacher stated she didn't know how she would have made it through that year without Millie's helpful attitude.

If you were abused by a teacher when you were young, it will be doubly painful for you to see your child suffer from similar words! Be sure, therefore, to work through your own earlier pain. This process—as explained in Chapter 15—takes time. Meanwhile try to separate yourself from your child so you can deal with her or him fairly and objectively.

Here are some specific actions you may choose to take in case your child is involved in verbal abuse at school.

1. Be certain your child is not the abuser. You will know the answer as you review how he or she treats you, the parent, and playmates in the neighborhood. If your child is guilty of verbal cruelty, I recommend that all the fun stops until the family has a serious talk about good manners. Establish a plan to teach courtesy and maintain an emphasis on kindness, instead of aggressiveness. Be sure to set an example, yourself.

The philosophy is understandable that unless you stand up for yourself, you will be abused. Children, however, commonly use this limited truth as an excuse to become bullies. Be careful to distinguish assertiveness from aggressiveness.

Assertiveness clarifies one's own needs and feelings without hurting another. *Aggressiveness* attacks others causing hurts and scars. The latter can easily become abuse.

If your child's teacher sounds abusive, try to determine if this is your child's perception or that of all the children in the class. Children are not above seeking their parents' sympathy by exaggerating a teacher's statements. Carefully avoid reinforcing such a habit if your child is indeed doing that. Talk with other parents, visit the classroom, and wait to see if your child reports problems consistently.

2. If you believe there really is verbal abuse, have a talk with the teacher. This is difficult and even risky, but you can do it. Avoid any attitude of over-protection of your child and seek an objective, positive approach. "Mrs. Jones," you might say, "I realize many children are rude and disobedient. I've observed them on my visits to school. I wonder if you realize that you, too, are rude at times. I suspect you may act that way to establish control. But it really hurts."

You must, of course, speak in your own words and style, but I have learned it is difficult for anyone to resist a helpful, kindly manner. While not always true, some teachers may appreciate your attempts to help, and you could make a difference.

3. If you meet with resistance, you may need to go on to the next step: get an appointment to speak clearly with your principal or higher authorities. Perhaps taking another parent or two with you would be helpful. Carefully avoid stirring up conflict and ask only other parents who have expressed concern independent of your influence. Again, be as positive as possible. Be specific with examples and have some constructive suggestions for change.

If time does not bring about the needed change, ask if

your child could be transferred to a different class. This step is risky because you can see there would be anarchy in schools if every child were moved when the going became tough.

Only if you have conclusive proof of genuine verbal abuse, go to your district superintendent and school board. Such action should be extremely rare, but there are occasional situations where it could prevent serious emotional damage to a number of children. If no action is taken, consider finding a private school. Such a move will be costly and perhaps you cannot afford it. If not, help your child accept the situation, stay out of trouble, and make it through the year. Keep a positive attitude and help your child avoid basic rebellion against all teachers and schools.

Education is legally required in America. Because of that fact, we sometimes forget what a privilege it is. As you teach your children the value of learning, you can help them transcend the difficult people who can make a classroom miserable for the students. To a certain degree, your child's future depends on doing so. Above all else, train and discipline your children to be respectful and kind. Be certain they do not retaliate with abuse of their own. Help your own family to be loving! Show them how!

✦ ✦ ✦

Study Questions

1. Describe any incidents of verbal abuse directed at you by a child. What kind of emotional damage resulted?

2. Without blame or accusation, how can you communicate with parents or teachers about a child's pattern of verbal abuse? What plan do you have for positive reinforcement and change, whether that child is a friend, a student, or your own?

3. What verbal abuse by teachers did you suffer as a child and how did it make you feel? In what ways do you think such abuse may have limited your academic or professional potential?

4. What steps can you take to work through such emotional damage and limited potential?

5. Do you have a child that you think may have suffered verbal abuse from a teacher? What positive steps can you take to clarify or correct this situation?

SEVEN

Profanity in the Pews

✦ ✦ ✦

S URELY ONE WOULD NOT FIND VERBAL ABUSE IN CHURCH!
There, one expects to find peace, forgiveness, and acceptance. Indeed such deep emotional and spiritual needs
can and often are found in churches. In fact, recent years
have shown a major increase in devotion to God and a
return to the practice of worship in America.

Yet, at the same time there is incredible verbal abuse in
God's house. This abuse can be heaped upon others by
what we say, both verbally and through body language.
Ignoring the obvious needs of others who worship right
next to us can inflict deep pain.

During the Gulf War, a Jewish friend shared her enor-
mous fear with me. Their daughter was living in Tel Aviv
during Iraq's scud attacks on that city. Both she and her
husband attended a large synagogue, well known for its wise
and compassionate leadership. They were actively involved
there and well known.

Sabbath after Sabbath, they attended services, voicing
their desperate concern for their child. They waited for
someone to ask about her welfare and share their worry.

Their fellow congregants were friendly, chatted amiably—even about the war. But not a soul asked about their loved one. Not one person uttered a word of sympathy or offered to pray for her safety. For my friend, those superficial chattering words that evaded her pain quickly became verbal abuse. The pain of neglecting to verbalize concern and comfort is another facet of abuse.

Our hedonistic world makes it easier to avoid pain than to share it. Abuse is often perpetrated by neglect and many churchgoers are guilty of such neglect. A multitude of social ills have become so commonplace that they no longer clutch at our hearts for attention. The pain of poverty is ignored, the injustices of our communities go unchallenged, and the isolation and loneliness of multiplied latch-key kids and single adults remains unaddressed. This unspoken abuse results in deep pain, leaving life-long scars and creating negative attitudes—and eventually, callouses.

CRUEL DISCIPLINE

Phil's mouth was dry and his palms were sweaty, yet he still shivered with a deep chill. His eyes brimmed with the tears he was trying to hold back, yet there was anger in his trembling voice. You see, Phil belonged to a church where any person who had been caught in a sin was required to confess that fault before the entire congregation. He had been a member there for several years and believed in their interpretations of the Bible. Now the time had come to face the music.

Phil had been caught having an affair. This needy, insecure man found his wife to be cold and critical. Desperate for loving acceptance, it seemed to come to him—as it so often does—from a young woman with whom he worked. At first, they spent coffee breaks innocently chatting together. They found such pleasure in these conversations that they began to go to lunch together. Soon it became easy to run an errand in the evenings where they could accidentally meet. Week by week, the infatuation grew until it blossomed into the poisonous flower of a full-blown affair.

Of course it was wrong. An affair never fixes a troubled marriage but hurts everyone instead. And when his infidelity was discovered, all of his wife's criticisms seemed suddenly justified. Phil had not *planned* this new relationship, but felt his needs had pushed him into the situation that just conveniently "happened." He had, however, chosen to go along with that push.

This church-going man loved God and feared the wrath of his punishment. When he and his hurt and angry wife met with the disciplinary committee of the church, Phil wordlessly accepted their verdict as if it were directly from God. "You are a sinner," they basically said, "and you must be punished. You must confess this secret sin before the entire congregation next Sunday morning."

Surely no one will ever know the monstrous shame and fear this young husband felt as he awaited that fateful day. Perhaps Phil found some strength in the belief that once confessed, his sins would go away. Then he might once again know peace of mind and be free of the guilt which plagued him. His troubled conscience and critical wife had made life unbearable. Perhaps she would forgive him after the coming ordeal.

The day came. The confession was made. The tears were shed. But the congregation seemed austere and ominously silent. After the service, no one came to shake Phil's hand, much less to embrace and forgive him. The relief and peace he so desperately needed were still missing. His wife's forgiveness was coldly absent.

Alone, Phil endured the day. Sleeplessly, he made it through the night. Silently, heroically he went to work on Monday as usual. And there she was! The one who had offered an escape from an unhappy marriage—now as remote and unreachable as a star in the sky. For him there was no hope, no joy, no love.

That evening, this distraught man loaded his gun, went back to the church, and stood in the spot where he had endured his public shame. There, alone, Phil shot himself. And there the pastor found him the next morning.

This church was guilty of verbal abuse as well as neglect. The members had pointed to him and hurled at him the stones of their blame. Many of them could excuse their own sins by accusing him. They themselves neglected to practice the biblical teachings of mercy, forgiveness, and the admission of their own sins. Despite the fact that his suicide was his own choice, how sad that Phil died alone, unforgiven.

Have you ever been verbally abused by your church? Phil needed correction—as do all of us who fall into waywardness of one kind or another. He was guilty of hurting his wife, his Christian witness, and his own spiritual life. When the Spirit of God convicts us of sin, true guilt motivates us to change, seek forgiveness, and be restored to wholeness. If you are in a church that fails to teach and practice mercy and forgiveness toward one who repents of sin, I suggest you begin an organized effort to change the negative attitudes. Meanwhile, study your Bible to discover the exciting news of restoration to wholeness.

NO WAY OUT

Impulsively and fiercely, Sarah threw her rosary as hard as her anger would reach. Symbolically, the crystal beads landed in a gutter where they silently reflected the late afternoon sun. For Sarah, there was no sun, no light at all.

This young woman was the oldest child in a devout Catholic family of six children. They never missed a service nor a ritual of their faith. Yet during the time they spent outside of church, some serious problems appeared. The father was preoccupied with showing his friends how much he could drink and how well he played cards. At home he was a tyrant, abusing both wife and children by his taunts and ridicule. When they winced or cried, he punished them, verbally and physically.

The mother was utterly drained by the painful demands of her life. Staying with her cruel husband and trying to stabilize their family had trapped her. Because of her religious beliefs and her own limitations, she could find no escape from the situation. To Sarah, her mother became the epitome of weakness, and she vowed to never become like her. Sarah was the one who stood up against the abuses of their alcoholic father, protecting her younger brothers and sisters the best she could. Even her mother learned to lean on the strength Sarah seemed to offer.

As soon as high school graduation was over, Sarah married her boyfriend as a welcome escape from the family trauma. At last she could be free of the unbearable burdens she had carried since early childhood. Soon, however, the sweetheart battles they had always weathered grew into explosive warfare. Sarah's father had been cruel, but Tony was a despot. His drinking episodes grew more frequent and longer lasting. Her life with him soon became unbearable.

In desperation, Sarah fled to her pastor. He listened to her tragic story—one with which he was all too familiar. But he felt bound by the religious laws and would not grant Sarah permission to leave her marriage vows. In a kindly effort to help, he offered suggestions that would enable her to get along with her tyrannical spouse.

Sarah felt she had tried all of these and none had helped. Knowing that all of her pleas for permission to get out of her marriage would be rejected by this clergyman, she still refused to live out her life in the painful pattern set by her mother.

In his own desperation, the pastor finally said, "Sarah, I

have nothing more to say. Just take this rosary and pray it every day." And with that he dismissed her. The man did not intend his words to be abusive, but to Sarah, they were extremely offensive. She felt they condemned her to choose between either a life that was unbearable or the departure from her life-long religious beliefs.

That day Sarah decided. She left both her faith and her husband, and entered a chapter of her life that was was marked by degradation and pain.

We could debate Sarah's story at length. Her pastor rightly needed to defend the standards in which he firmly believed. Yet her family history of verbal abuse had left her extremely vulnerable to what she perceived to be a new attack. She had already been injured emotionally and spiritually. The impact of what she perceived as unbending rigidity on the part of this clergyman resulted only in further hurt—as well as her departure from her faith and the end of any future opportunity her pastor may have had to help her.

We cannot resolve the question of divorce in this book. The indissolubility of sacramental marriage remains central to the teaching of some historic churches. The annulment procedure that is allowed by them is an attempt to bring justice and compassion to those whose marriage was one in appearance only. We cannot judge the merits of this particular instance for ourselves. But the important point for our consideration is that Sarah failed to receive the kind of compassionate help she so desperately needed in coping with her abusive marriage.

If you need understanding and help from your pastor, but find little, let me suggest that you follow these steps.

1. Continue to visit on several occasions, trying to understand their point of view as well as your own needs.
2. Clarify both your issues and what you hear them saying—enabling them to understand that they are somehow missing the mark with you. If their words cause

you pain without help or healing, tell them so. And ask simply for what you need. Do remember that tough, honest love may hurt at the moment, but gives insight and correction in the long run!

3. If your pastor cannot help you, look around for another counselor who may be more specifically attuned to your unique needs. Above all, do not toss out your faith in God along with your loss of confidence in your minister. That was Sarah's biggest mistake. God's wisdom, love, and protection are your source of power!

POWER STRUGGLES

Many times I have observed that churches are dysfunctional in ways that are remarkably similar to what can go wrong in biological families. The struggle for power, the feelings of resentment, and the bitterness of verbal abuse and retaliation—all these human foibles are lurking behind even minor disagreements. Sibling rivalry is reenacted by members who feel someone else is gaining too much recognition or power. Someone always loses during such battles, but those who apparently win will also lose if they have conquered through verbal abuse.

Let me illustrate. A growing church was ready to enlarge its building. Several possibilities for doing so emerged, and as time elapsed opinions regarding the best option inevitably became strongly divergent. The differences in the actual plans seemed very important at first, but they became miniscule compared to the upset feelings of both warring factions.

As so universally happens in power struggles, everyone lost sight of what would be best suited to the needs of the people. Instead, the focus rested on who could win this contest of wills. Committee meetings became battle grounds. In the church foyers and at social events, people separated into whispering clusters who glanced malevolently at each other. Those who refused to take sides did not know who was the enemy. Bitter accusations shot like bullets between the two groups, each volley escalating in intensity over the last.

Such fighting, of course, had to reach an end. And so did this battle. But in the end, it left ugly wounds in the spirits of the losers. The manipulative manner in which the victors won had destroyed their trust. Many of them, hurt to the quick, eventually left the church. Those who stayed carefully avoided contact with their opponents. Suspicion and sullen resentments crippled the growth of this congregation for a long time. Verbal abuse in the church can be a deadly force, killing the spirit, not only of individuals, but even the church itself.

Another church was so crowded that newcomers felt as if they were a nuisance. The building lacked enough space for the various programs and even parking space was becoming a major problem. There would need to be a change. Should the church close its doors in the city and move to the suburbs? Or should it give birth to a new church, thereby risking the division of its members? Certainly, the answer to this dilemma was not an easy one.

The governing board of this particular congregation used a democratic process in which all the members had both a voice and a vote. The debates grew more and more heated in the numerous meetings. A young father of a small baby stood to speak his opinion and earnestly stated his concern for his child. As she grew up, Gene hoped his daughter might be a member of this church, relocated near the school she would attend. He stated that he would like to see the congregation relocate and continue to grow for the sake of his children.

An older man rose next. Arnold had been one of the founders of the existing church, a recognized authority in its leadership. He valued its long history and was firmly opposed to seeing it move. This man was also accustomed to having his way. He would be happy to gain the advantage courteously, but was well known for his caustic words when he deemed them necessary.

Dramatically, Arnold reviewed the history of the existing building, the sacrifice required to build it, the role this church had played in so many of their lives as individuals and families. This historic building should, of course, never close. Then he added, addressing the young father, "Gene, you're just a young kid. What do you know? You've never been a part of the struggles to build this church. You're only a novice, fresh out of school. Leave the big decision to those who have experience!" Arnold's face revealed the disdain he felt for the young man. His tone of voice emphatically put him down.

Gene's words, however, had appealed to the sizeable group of younger families who had gradually enlarged this church. They agreed with his wish to have a church near their homes, one that could grow and influence their community. The vote finally came and Gene's words influenced the decision to move to a growing young community. Arnold's power had finally been broken. But most of those young, eager parishioners never forgot the rancor of his words. Verbal abuse may not always result in disaster, but it always leaves emotional scars—and frequently scars of the spirit.

Many of you women have suffered another source of spiritual abuse—the custom tenaciously held in many church groups of excluding you from various areas of ministry in your churches. With frequent insensitivity, women's varied gifts and insights are all too often ignored by male-dominated leadership, except to encourage the performance of the most menial tasks.

The first book I wrote was co-authored with a clergyman, the pastor of a large church. He invited me to visit his church and to "say a few words" regarding the content and concerns we shared about youth. To his personal embarrassment, however, he was forbidden by his board to allow me to speak from the platform. I had to stand at the lowest level of the auditorium where I could not see the back of the building.

I was mature enough to cope with that humiliation, but the experience enabled me to sympathize with my Christian sisters. Many of you have an intense desire to teach or otherwise serve God in your churches. You have much to offer, but you find the doors are shut. I know this feeling of helplessness causes deep pain. The unfairness and unreasonableness you sometimes encounter can embitter you if you allow it.

Once again, you do have choices! Let me suggest some helpful avenues you might explore in improving this situation.

1. You can always continue to practice your faith and study your Bibles. You will find a number of examples of women in Scripture who were given respect and opportunities for service. Tell your church leaders lovingly about these women.
2. Seek others who share your interests or sense of "calling" and go as a group to those who establish your church's policies. Repeatedly and in love, urge them to consider your ideas.
3. Practice the quality of patience. Many changes have taken place in recent years. Good changes that take place slowly are usually lasting. There certainly is a healthy balance to be found in assertiveness and patience. Each of you must find your own place along that spectrum.
4. While you wait, look for opportunities to demonstrate your positive attitude. And continually be alert to areas of service for God that will utilize your spiritual gifts.

5. Find a godly mentor—a woman who shares your eagerness and understands your frustrations. She needs to be mature and stable enough to guide you in this highly risky journey!

6. Remember that human beings are always limited in their knowledge. God, alone, is unlimited. So go to him consistently for the gentle strength, guidance, and wisdom you need.

ANSWERS TO CONFLICT AND ABUSE

During the conflicts inherent in power struggles, much verbal abuse is exchanged. As we have seen, places of worship are certainly not immune from this difficulty. Churchgoers are as imperfect as anyone else. The answers to such confusing issues and the dynamics involved, however, are not so difficult to find at a personal level. Here is a list of suggestions in dealing with conflict and abuse.

1. Keep in mind the tendency in every human being to first want his or her own way, and then to retaliate when winning is impossible. Remember that people who speak abusive words are unconsciously trying to find and express a degree of power. Almost always, they feel power*less* and thus go overboard trying to feel power*ful.*

2. You have the power to choose how you receive abusive words—either as a personal insult or as the expression of a power-hungry individual. You may even become so mature that you can feel a degree of compassion for the underlying weakness of such insecure abusers.

3. Set an example by refusing to retaliate or join any attack on a given faction. Instead, stay objective and try to help others stick with the most basic issue: "What is in the best interests of the most people involved in this situation?"

4. As you learn to recognize, understand, and forgive abusive persons, you will be mastering the methods for achieving healing for other areas of abuse in your life. Be encouraged that *you* can be effective in stopping factional abuses in your church and even instrumental in promoting healing!

✦ ✦ ✦

Study Questions

1. Describe any painful incidents of silence or neglect on the part of fellow church members regarding a difficult situation in your life.

2. Have you ever been publicly disciplined before your congregation for some fault or sin? If so, describe the incident and your feelings surrounding such an experience.

3. What kind of shame and guilt do you carry because of failing to live up to unrealistic expectations of a religious group?

4. In what ways have you ever been verbally abused by your minister or failed to receive help and support in times of distress?

5. Have you rejected your parents' church tradition because of such hurt and rejection? If yes, describe this situation and the emotional scars you bear.

6. How have damaging power struggles within a church or religious organization affected you? In what ways have you felt disdained or manipulated by those in the congregation or religious organization with greater influence?

7. If you are a woman, have you ever felt unfairly excluded from various areas of ministry? If yes, describe the situations and how you responded.

In the Marketplace

✦ ✦ ✦

VERBAL ABUSE DOES NOT WORK IN marriages, families, schools, or churches. Neither will it work on the job, even though it is extremely common there.

Ours is an era of independent, even rebellious people in the work force. Many of them will walk off the job and live on the streets rather than take verbal abuse from an employer. Most of these people have suffered abuse from others and feel they no longer have to submit to such practices. I suspect some of the growing number of "street people" could become loyal employees if one knew how to teach them gently and deal kindly with their mistakes.

Even in more complex jobs, I have observed harsh supervisors being subtly sabotaged by their abused staff. And the atmosphere of any organization ultimately reflects the attitude of its top boss. If he or she rules with threats and criticism, the entire staff reflects and re-enacts that reign of fear. The end product is an angry work force who perform far below their potential.

Wherever you are, fight against such a negative environment. Maintain your own inner sense of kindness, understanding, and caring. Counteract harshness with these positive qualities and your own standards of excellence. At least you yourself will be happier and less vulnerable to the abuses. Just maybe, you can influence one or two others who might change one or two others! Every little bit helps.

FEELING UNNEEDED

Large corporations may be expected to grow impersonal, cold, and even abusive. But smaller organizations are not at all immune to such abusive trends. Let me give you an example. One company began to lose employees to better salaries elsewhere. Job opportunities were plentiful at the time and security was less important than money. This business, while solid, could not possibly compete with new and larger corporations. All of their efforts to create additional benefits and better working conditions were ineffective in slowing down the inexorable exodus.

The head of that organization eventually began to see the steady stream of resignations as a personal affront to himself. Remember, it is often out of one's own pain that verbal abuse erupts. And so it happened to the people involved here. The loyal top employees attended regular management meetings. At one of these, the head officer discussed the loss of employees and his interpretation of this steady trend.

Filled with the pent-up hurt and rage of weeks past, he loudly condemned the lack of loyalty, failure to appreciate his efforts, and general inadequacies of the greedy folks who worked more for money than for altruistic reasons. After several moments of waxing hot in his statements, this poor man yelled, "I don't know who'll leave next. And frankly, I don't care! It may be some of you or all of you. If you're greedy, go ahead and leave. Who needs you, anyway? We don't need any of you!"

Once again, you can see the pitiful core of these abusive words. Fear, pain, and his own weakness and needs had transformed this otherwise good employer into a tyrant. Anger and defiance had made him feel a deceptive sense of power. Actually, he was a strong man, capable in many ways. But his character evidenced the fatal flaw of taking people's simple, understandable failings as a personal insult. He could not stomach the pain of that rejection without trying to protect himself by hurling his abusive words toward even loyal and innocent bystanders.

Each of us who have worked in the business or professional world may recall those kinds of painful verbal attacks. Perhaps you have been treated in much worse ways than the examples related here. Many instances have racial as well as sexist implications. Indeed, sexual harassment is becoming more and more commonly reported. You may have allowed yourself to become bitter and vindictive because of such abuse. Or you may have found the abuse so defeating that you have given up, ending up far below your best potential because you came to believe the insults.

Take another look. Perhaps it is not you at all, but the abuser who is inadequate. We'll describe in the last part of this book how you can put such defeat or bitterness behind you and find a joy-filled and successful new future. "Today is the first day of the rest of your life!"

NEVER ENOUGH

In all kinds of work and at all levels, stress sometimes runs high, tempers become short, and verbal abuse flares up. In few areas is this fact more true than in medicine. And in all the complex branches of medicine, few are more likely to be victims of such abuse than are interns. Nurses certainly run a close second, and at this point in time may even be the number one victims.

I speak from personal experience. In my era, after four years of medical school, all of us served a full year of time rotating through all the major medical specialties. We worked under the careful supervision of the resident doctors, the staff physicians, the nurses, and just about all the other disciplines. We took advice, lectures, and blame from almost everyone, felt quite unsure of ourselves and were extremely vulnerable.

During my year as an intern, I learned and grew under such an environment, knowing for a certainty that I had to either sink or swim. In fact I endured the long days and on-call nights so well that I earned an award at the end of that seemingly endless year. My professional abilities, however, did not spare me from one of the worst tongue-lashings I have ever received.

It happened on a Sunday evening after a hectic weekend. I had worked without ceasing for over thirty-six hours with only a few hours of sleep. One of the staff obstetricians came to see a patient of his who had delivered a new baby and was doing well. Some obscure laboratory test he had ordered had been overlooked—not by me, but by another doctor. I happened to be standing near him and had been on call, so he assumed I was at fault.

For at least ten minutes—which seemed fully two hours—this angry physician railed at me in a loud voice. In front of all the nurses, aides, maids, lab technicians, and other interns, he shouted about my stupidity and laziness. He worried about whatever hospital might be stuck with such an incompetent doctor.

When I tried to explain the truth of the situation, he rudely refused to listen. Even my attempt at a dishonest apology failed to calm his rage. He simply screamed until he ran out of adrenaline and voice. This guy then turned his back on me and stomped furiously down the hall, leaving me feeling utterly powerless.

Hot tears welled up in my eyes and I wanted to run—

either after him to make him listen or into some closet to hide from my humiliation. I could do neither. Eventually I recovered. Some of the adjacent staff offered comfort and excellent advice. The nurses, so commonly the targets of many doctors' displaced frustrations, certainly understood. One of my dear fellow interns put into some pithy words what I should have said! The event passed; I continued to grow and learn—but not from that abusive man. The memory of the pain he inflicted is vivid even some thirty-eight years later.

The tragedy of verbal abuse lies in its triple effect.

1. Its direct target is devastated.
2. Those who overhear such remarks are placed in a position of judging both persecutor and victim.
3. The explosion leaves the perpetrator with guilt and growing callouses.

I later learned that this doctor who had given me the tongue-lashing was an alcoholic who had already lost the respect of most of the staff. He had become so calloused over the years that he no longer cared—not about others' feelings, not even about his own character.

Sadly, this troubled, sick man felt as if he had won in this confrontation. I had been rendered helpless, humiliated in front of my peers, and reduced to tears. Yet in the long run, he was the loser. You may be sure I avoided him as much as possible without depriving his patients of good care. The other staff added one more link of disdain for him to the long chain they already had. And perhaps, in some hidden, tiny pocket of his heart, he, too, realized how monstrous his behavior really was.

For many years, nurses have suffered frequent rebuffs and abuse from physicians. During tense moments in surgery, emergency rooms, and baby deliveries, I have heard multitudes of abusive comments, labels, and tirades. Because of the code of ethics then in effect, nurses had to take such verbal attacks in silence. Any retaliatory comments could result in their being fired for "insubordination."

Small wonder, then, that nurses finally decided enough was enough. In more or less silent rebellion, they stopped the dramatic "respect" they had once been forced to act out. They no longer stand at "attention" when a physician comes into sight, and they often leave doctors to their own devices while they are busy elsewhere. And who can blame them? In recent years, I have seen many healthy improvements in doctor-nurse relationships.

But abuse begets abuse. Once again, the instinctive retaliation principle is demonstrated. The very people who have taken abuse learn to give it with multiplied force. On one occasion I was pressed beyond endurance with the many tasks I had to complete. In the midst of those demands, I needed to squeeze in a physical examination for a young woman. I had called ahead and explained to the nurse my time constraints and asked that she have the patient and equipment ready at the only time I had available. The nurse agreed to do so.

When I arrived at the examining room breathless and anxious about my next appointment, I found my patient fully dressed and reading a book. With the most patience I could muster—but with the irritation my predicament generated—I asked the nurse why the patient was not ready. Lilly was new in our hospital and I was unprepared for her tirade.

"You doctors are all alike!" she berated me. "You think you are God Almighty and can tell everyone what to do. I want you to know I will get this patient gowned when I'm good and ready and then only because I choose—not because you tell me to!"

The tirade of this nurse, who had almost certainly been abused by other doctors, seemed to echo the abusive physician from my past. I was getting it from both sides. As I listened to Lilly's caustic words, I realized that I had come a long way since my internship. Certainly her words stung my heart and brought consternation to my mind. But promptly I realized that I was not, this time, the victim.

I knew I had not been rude to her and that I did not deserve her anger. I had matured enough to see that Lilly was dumping on me the pent-up hurt and rage she had accumulated from others. She was taking no risks that I should join forces with those others. This time, she would take the offensive.

For me to become angry and retaliate was not only useless but unnecessary. Instead, I postponed the procedure, relieved the pressure on my day, and was able to gain the composure only time and experience can give. I must add, however, that I never regained my original respect for this woman!

You see, when you must be on the receiving end of abuse, you do have a choice. You can feel helpless, hurt, and sad, or you may become angry and retaliate. Some years ago, a comic phrase made the rounds: "Don't get mad; get even!" Thankfully, neither is necessary. Again, I remind you—you can transcend the abusive situation by insight into the sickness of the abuser and even some degree of compassion for his or her dysfunction.

SEXUAL HARASSMENT

Sexual statements once taken for granted as acceptable jokes are not funny. Very recently an early evening national TV show depicted a macho sheriff saying to a young woman as he fumbled with his pants zipper, "Your problem is you've never had the love of a good man!" She was being unjustly held in his jail and was totally at his mercy. Fortunately the drama revealed him to be the rascal he really was and showed his prompt removal from office.

In real life, the story does not always end so well. News-papers in my own city reveal that public officials from county offices to national officials are often accused and found guilty of sexual aggression as well as sexist statements. A large city newspaper described events in which a state attorney general paid a sizeable sum of money to the victim of his verbal abuse. Yet he remained in office and was even re-elected. This woman had worked with the man and decided she did not have to take his ribald comments.

Several years ago I conducted a number of seminars for some large corporations. As I learned about their inner workings, I became saddened at the stories of the staff. There were many such tales, but two stand out as prime examples.

The first concerned a woman we'll call Amanda. She was tall, typically dressed for success, both intelligent and charming. Surely Amanda could make it to the top as well as anyone—male or female. But she sadly did not believe in herself and felt she could win promotions only by manipu-lating and game playing.

Amanda was elated when the senior vice president asked to see her in his office. He was highly complimentary of her work and assured her she had a great future with the com-pany. He asked if she would like to work with him on a big project that was being planned. Ever so subtly, he indicated that the work might demand some travel. Could she be away now and then for a few days? Could she? Amanda jumped at the opportunity!

Amanda believed her boss really felt she was a capable employee. She worked hard to gain his approval, and he was not easily pleased. For a number of weeks, she ignored and overlooked his occasional winks and personal tone of voice. After all, she knew she was attractive, but she also knew he was married. A few more weeks and a number of lunches and dinners passed. The clever man implied that he would like to be more than her employer and friend.

Abruptly Amanda realized his game and knew she should have faced those overlooked signs long ago. While this young woman uncomfortably tried to reason out her possible options, she was horrified to hear, "Amanda, I like you. You're pretty good. But unless you're interested in an intimate relationship, frankly, I have little to offer you. There are others who are as good at the job as you." The voice, while still courteous, was edged in coolness and painted with the glitter of his official power.

It could well be debated that these powerful words were not abusive. But I contend they were. They clearly implied a put-down of this employee's work and ability. They created a degree of helplessness because her refusal would mean a major downgrade in rank and pay. While pretending some affection, Amanda was not naive enough to believe this ruthless man really loved her. He was using her and had carefully groomed her to be vulnerable to his ultimate focus—a new sexual object.

Amanda had worked so hard and had begun to think of herself as top management material. Well, she hastily decided, she had come too far to turn back now. She would play his game and win the position she coveted. And so she did. Amanda determined that night that she would accept his offer and play his game. In fact, she thought, I may just beat him at his own game. I can threaten later to reveal this man's abusiveness, if he fails to give me the raises I need.

The corporate world, I'm told, is all too familiar with such verbal abuse. Sexual harassment is becoming well-defined and can now result in dismissing the perpetrator. But like Amanda's situation, some carefully laid plans are so well constructed that women see no way out.

Yet, in fact, there are ways out. And Connie's story makes them clear. She was a good saleswoman for another large corporation. No matter how hard she tried, she had not been able to gain a coveted management position. Several times she applied, each time documenting her efforts and her top qualifications. She knew she was as good as her competitors—who all happened to be men.

Once more that coveted spot was going to be open for a new bid. Connie carefully updated her resumé, practiced her interview skills, and collected endorsements. When the day of the interview arrived, she entered the office of her potential new boss with a certain optimism. After the usual pleasantries, this man fell silent and looked at Connie. She squirmed inwardly as she recognized the implications of that look.

Could he really be so blatant, she wondered? "Connie, you've applied for this job three times. Obviously you want to work for me. I'd be glad to have you, but frankly, it is likely to involve a serious relationship with me. I find you attractive and we'll have plenty of opportunities for discreet meetings. How about it?"

This man had underestimated Connie. She was both courageous and capable, and she did not hesitate in turning down his offer. She would stay in sales forever rather than prostitute herself for a promotion. Furthermore, she would let his offer be known at the proper time to the appropriate people.

Connie's character was strong enough to reject the abuse that would have made her only one more sex object, a pawn in the competitive corporate world. She simply shed his words and their implication—directly aimed at her, but once again, reflective of her boss' own pathetic inadequacy.

Today's American TV viewers will not soon forget the fight between the Honorable Clarence Thomas and attorney Anita Hill. Mr. Thomas, nominated by President Bush for the highest honor an attorney in this country may know, was being accused of sexual harrassment by Ms. Hill. Friends and co-workers of both of these outstanding people led all of America in taking sides with one against the other.

One hopes that from such conflict, there might emerge a greater sense of empathy for women by men—and a greater sense by women of the vulnerability of men as well as women. Instead of greater mutual understanding, however, we are experiencing more animosity on both sides as the battle of the sexes escalates.

Maureen is a classic example of true sexual harassment. She is a shy and charming young wife, conscientious in her work and a woman of great integrity. Yet a middle-aged male in a position of greater responsibility than she, began to hang around her desk. If she moved to a different area to work, he found her and made excuses to chat. He tried to touch her and knowingly looked at her attractive body in ways that made her squirm.

This young woman maintained her dignity at all times. She carefully avoided being alone with him and never left work except with a trusted co-worker. Those who know Maureen all agreed that she did everything in her power to avoid the offenses of this man. In spite of her sensitive efforts, he pursued her inviting her to go out with him "just for a drink."

At last Maureen, unable to tolerate being near such an obnoxious person, went to his superior. She revealed the harassment she had suffered and described her efforts to cope. She gave the names of fellow workers who could verify the facts and were willing to do so.

The man refused to change his behavior, even when warned by his supervisor. In a few weeks, he was dismissed. Not only did Maureen win her struggle for the right to privacy and dignity, but also she won greater safety for all the women in her office.

Not every incident turns out so well, but this example depicts precisely the steps to take if you are being sexually harassed.

1. She evidenced her own absolute and total commitment to appropriate and professional values and behavior.

2. She tried by actions, words, and attitudes to stop this man's pursuit of her.
3. She avoided risky or even questionable situations, at work and outside of work.
4. She avoided any and all double messages.
5. When, in a reasonable time, her efforts failed to stop him, she reported this man to the appropriate authorities in a clear, unemotional appeal for help.

If you are in a comparable situation, remember the steps you can take. You are not helpless! Be sure you take a stand to protect yourself and support others who also encounter harassment.

❖ ❖ ❖

Study Questions

1. What specific incidents of verbal abuse by supervisors or employers can you recall? How did you feel at the time and how did you respond?

2. How has a negative work environment characterized by threat and criticism or being made to feel unwanted or unneeded at work damaged your sense of self-worth? What can you do to change such a situation?

3. Have you ever experienced the shame and humiliation of a tongue-lashing in front of others about real or perceived mistakes on the job? If so, describe the incidents.

4. What specific incidents of verbal abuse from co-workers can you recall?

5. As the victim of abuse, how did you respond? By feeling helpless, hurt, or sad? By becoming angry and retaliating in kind? Or by realizing your abuser was unjustly dumping on you and having compassion on his or her dysfunction?

6. Describe any incidents of subtle or overt sexual harassment at work. How did this make you feel? How did you respond? Was your response appropriate? If not, what could you do differently?

NINE

Living in an Irate World

✦ ✦ ✦

WE LIVE IN A WORLD FILLED WITH the stress of deadlines and too much to do in a given amount of time. This constant stress often erupts as we try to make our way through all of the hustle and bustle. Sometimes we are on the receiving end of the resulting abuse; sometimes we help to dish it out. Let's look at some examples of this all too common occurrence.

Traveling is an endlessly changing kaleidoscope of experiences. When we are necessarily caught on this treadmill, some of our experiences are funny, some are sad, a few are frightening, and many are maddening. Among those maddening ones are the transactions between harassed ticket agents and frustrated travelers. (Since I travel mainly by air, my examples are related to airports. But I feel confident these situations are duplicated in bus and train depots as well.)

It happens in Dallas, Atlanta, Indianapolis, Denver, Kansas City, Albuquerque, Seattle, and San Francisco. It happens in every airport at some time. A plane is late and a connection to another flight is missed. A flight is overbooked and not enough seats are available for everyone who purchased tickets. Not only is a plane late, but last week a plane was out of repair and the flight was cancelled. The unsuspecting passengers were never even notified.

Recently, such a near-catastrophe happened to me. I was scheduled to speak to a group in a large church in the South. They had planned this event months in advance and had spent a great deal of money advertising it. The small plane that was to take me from a metropolitan airport to my destination was listed at the last moment as being twenty minutes late. This small delay certainly posed no problem, but when that time arrived, another delay was posted.

I looked out the window and could see the parked commuter planes scattered about the airport. As one after another plane departed, I noticed to my horror large pieces of one engine of *my* plane lying on the ground. Like magnets they fixed my gaze, as minute after precious minute ticked by. At last I realized that plane could not leave in time to reach my destination.

As I approached the young ticket agent at the departure area, I could not help but hear a very angry passenger berating him. He recounted a number of times in recent weeks when some unforeseen problem had ruined his commuter flight. The ticket agent was obviously not a mechanic nor a manager, but had to endure several moments of serious verbal abuse from this inconvenienced and irate passenger.

Finally, the poor abuser left and I had to accost the same abused agent. I gently explained the urgency of my mission. "When," I asked, "is there another flight? Is there some other airline that could get me to my appointment? Could I rent a car and drive there?" This time I became the target, as the hapless young man showered upon me his frustration with the previous passenger.

After he assured me that he didn't know (and obviously didn't care!), he referred me down a long corridor with a disgusted wave of his hand. Fortunately, there I found a young woman who was not only helpful but kind as well. By a miracle, I made my destination barely in time. And so did my angry fellow traveler. But how much happier we all could have been in those difficult moments had no one become abusive. I have seen this scenario acted out with multitudinous variations over many years. And so have many of you. Perhaps you have, at times, been an abuser!

Let me make some suggestions that can help you through similar tense times in your travels. Apart from allowing more time by taking earlier departures, here are some suggestions for coping with verbally abusive people.

1. In the midst of an angry encounter with a ticket agent, try to place yourself in the other person's shoes. Imagine the stress he or she lives with—not just at this moment, but hour after hour and day after day. Such a job requires taking abuse regularly. Fortunately I heard this agent's encounter with a fellow traveler, so I knew I need not take his abuse personally.
2. When you are in a position similar to mine, try a comment to the person about the abuse you overheard. Offer a word of understanding or comfort. This accomplishes two wonderful objectives. First, it places you securely in a strong and healthy position to be able to comfort another person. Second, it becomes nearly impossible for that man or woman to abuse you and several more people to follow.
3. Make a firmer commitment to avoid ever being guilty of such abuse yourself.

THE HORRORS OF SHOPPING

Similar encounters are not uncommon in large retail stores. While in high school and college, I worked in many such stores to help pay the costs of my education. I was carefully trained and diligently supervised to know that "the cus-tomer is always right." I was made aware that the very exis-tence of the store—and therefore my job—depended on the good will of their customers.

As a shopper, I was not at all prepared for the behavior and attitudes of many department store employees. On one typical occasion, I found two young salespeople after having extensively and unsuccessfully searched for a particular item on my own. I needed help to find the correct depart-ment and sizes of clothing for my new grandson. As a proud grandmother, I was happily anticipating the purchase and its effect on this recent addition to my daughter's family.

But these employees were interested in only one thing: an animated conversation about the latest dates they'd had. I waited several moments and interjected several exclama-tions of "Excuse me, please!" One of them finally managed to stop chattering long enough to offhandedly point to a rack packed with children's garb. I had already carefully examined that rack and found it to lack the sort of item I needed.

By the time I glanced in the direction she had pointed and back again, these girls had already returned to their animated conversation. I must admit my own voice was tinged with some sarcasm as I intruded again into their con-versation. "If it's not too much trouble, would one of you please be able to help me? Here's what I need." And I tried to describe clearly the sleepers for which I was looking.

Actually that particular garment was near the rack she had gestured toward, so she said sullenly, "See! They're right here where I told you they were!" I was able to ignore her rudeness and finally received the help I needed to locate my purchases.

Perhaps this example is one of rudeness more than out-right abuse. But actually, is rudeness itself not verbal abuse? Let's examine this issue more closely as illustrated by these sales clerks. First their behavior and attitudes clearly shouted, "You, customer, are not important. We and our interests are what count!" Next, her words implied that I must be blind and stupid to not be able to follow the wave of her hand. Her facial expression, tone of voice, and actions said, "I don't like to be bothered with you. Help your own self." This incident has lasted in my memory and makes me reluctant to enter that store again. Another emotional scar, even though a tiny one, has been added to my collection.

This example reiterates the chain reaction of verbal abuse—or rudeness, if you will. I am acutely aware of verbal abuse and consciously work hard to avoid committing it. Yet here I was, in front of these seemingly shallow, certainly inconsiderate young women with sarcasm in my own voice and resentment in my heart.

With any lesser resolve to be kind most of the time, I could have retaliated in fine style. I might have even tried to see to it that they lost their jobs. You can see the far-reaching influence of using words that hurt with an attitude that multiplies the pain! Whenever you experience such pain, let that prompt you to choose even more firmly to avoid retaliating.

On another occasion, a friend and I were just parking to enter a restaurant when a healthy young person parked adjacent to our car. The space was clearly marked as reserved for handicapped people. So as I reached the curb, I politely asked the driver if she realized that parking space was reserved. I have often failed to notice a worn sign designating such parking, so I assumed she also might have missed it. I feel strongly that persons with handicaps need special consideration.

I am certain I was not impolite, so I was totally unprepared for her explosion. "What's it to you, old woman?" she asked. "Mind your own damn business!" And then she nearly pushed me aside as she strode into the very restaurant we were entering. To my shock—and finally amusement—she donned the uniform of a waitress. As my friend and I were seated, we realized she was working in our area. I observed her speak to the manager who assigned another person to our table. By her face, I suspect she was a bit ashamed of her treatment and too embarrassed to wait on us.

Obviously, this girl was late to work, deliberately parked in the first vacant spot, and was angry about being confronted. Perhaps I should have minded my own business, but one way I try to combat abuse is by staying committed to caring about people who have special needs. Perhaps my comment to her will make her more thoughtful in the future. At any rate, if we are to protect ourselves and others in our world from all kinds of abuse, we must take some risks. I'm glad I did!

On another shopping trip, I was waiting in line for several moments to make my purchases. The two people behind the cash register were talking about their manager, as I could hear all too clearly. They described what she wore, how she had acted, and exactly how many drinks she had imbibed at last evening's party. I fidgeted and cleared my throat, but they were not to be disturbed. They derogated the way she managed the store and the merchandise she stocked.

When at last they finished, one did wait on me in a friendly manner. I appreciated that. But I had observed several other customers look at the two in disgust and walk out. I like to see small, independent businesses succeed, and I knew such behavior would not exactly build any customer's confidence.

I decided to risk another effort to counter abusive words. In the gentlest possible way, I quietly commented on the facts I have just described and suggested that customers liked to know positive facts about a store. The young person looked amazed and startled me by her reply. "Gosh! You're right. I didn't realize we were talking so loud. You're really nice for telling me. I appreciate it."

Once in a while, a positive, kindly spoken reaction against

verbal abuse—even when directed toward another person—may prove helpful. We dare not stop trying to counteract it!

IT'S A MAN'S WORLD

Sometimes verbal abuse grows out of outgrown misperceptions. One example lies in the role assigned to women as being generally subservient to men. Servanthood is a special calling and various people, both male and female, respond to such a call in their own corners of the world. It takes a strong, caring, well-balanced person to serve others in a healthy way.

Many people, however, believe that only a woman can make coffee or serve as the secretary of a committee. They seem to perceive these jobs not as a healthy, voluntary position of service, but as only slightly better than slavery!

I have worked as a physician in a variety of disciplines for nearly four decades. During my internship I vividly recall a snowy day when many hospital staff could not get to work. I realized the predicament of the nursing staff so I immediately pitched in to help. We all changed linens, cleaned bathrooms, and helped give baths. It felt really good to help out and serve both staff and patients. It was fun to forget I was "the doctor" and just be a person who was available to serve in whatever tasks needed to be done.

Recently, however, I served as the "token" woman on an institutional board in my vicinity. I had gladly shared my ideas and not one of them had been used. My interest in the particular institution was genuine, and I gave freely of my time and involvement. Yet little appreciation was ever expressed. The men on the board were just not accustomed to viewing a woman as a very intelligent person and equal peer.

I was willing to try to teach them the value of a woman's unique perceptions and insights. The day inevitably came, however, when the usual secretary was unable to attend the meeting. The chairman looked around the table and said, "Grace, you are the only woman here, could you serve as our secretary?" I took a bit of perverse delight in my answer. "No," I replied, "my physician's scrawl would be unreadable. I'm afraid I'm no good at taking notes."

I hope you understand clearly the points involved in this story. These men had invited me to join this board as a professional equal, then had consistently ignored my input at all levels. Yet when they found a task *they* saw as characteristically beneath them, they did not hesitate to ask me to pitch in. These thoughtless men had suddenly revealed their own prejudices.

Let me say emphatically that I do not feel a secretary is inferior. I myself could not function without the dear friends who are my secretaries. That role is very valuable and essential. Neither have I ever shrunk from being a willing servant. During all of my school years, I had worked conscientiously at a variety of jobs, including scrubbing floors, doing laundry, and caring for children. But I was unwilling to accept this perhaps unwitting relegation of me to the role *these men* saw as inferior. I chuckle even now, as I recall the secret delight I enjoyed at declining.

Verbal abuse may not be actively rude or even angry. Often it is an unconscious categorization that robs the victim of his or her dignity as a person. You can instantly see how widespread such putdowns are regarding racial and ethnic groups, as well as women.

VICIOUS GOSSIP

The most enjoyable social experiences I know are those shared with a few trusted friends or even just one special person. And the best friends of all are the members of my own family. But many times I find it necessary to be in large parties with relative strangers. I have learned a great deal by observing and listening. Here are some examples of what I've discovered.

One is that it is never okay for two women to wear identical dresses. Two very wealthy women I know unwittingly made this error. I could not miss the look of chagrin on each of their faces when they realized this "terrible" mistake. As I overheard the whispered comments of other ladies, I understood why this was such a serious circumstance. It was suggested they must have shopped in cheap stores, implying that perhaps they were suffering financial reverses!

No matter what the dress style, what women wear seems to be open to criticism. If it's cut too low or too short, the wearer is a brazen hussy. If it's too simple and severe, she is a prude. And such statements, often spoken in loud whispers, obviously leave off describing the dress and address the speaker's judgment of the woman. Many times the abusive words come from the pit of jealousy rather than any personal knowledge. Such judgments, even if they are true, are never useful. They are verbal abuse, as is all gossip.

Even casual friendliness with a member of the opposite sex may be judged as a play for someone's spouse. True enough, flirtations and frank affairs are painfully frequent these days. But idle judgments of social interactions are cruelly abusive. If such accusations are true, gossip only feeds the flames of such a tawdry, grievous fact. If they are not true, the pain of doubt and suspicion will certainly invade the mind and heart of the spouse. Don't ever say such careless words and don't listen to them without challenging their veracity. This stand will not make you popular, but it will give you respect and a chance to help stop verbal abuse.

Gossipy comments about an individual's job, children, financial stability, or marriage are very often not true. I once heard that small minds focus primarily on things; average minds on people; and great minds on ideas. I would like to add that abusive gossip flows from idle or careless people. Yet at social affairs—especially where alcoholic beverages are plentiful—endless, heart-breaking examples of verbal abuse through gossip abound. The aftermath of many of these idle comments is the increase in superficial, role-playing interactions among a large segment of our world.

Such sad social abuses occur at all levels of economic, intellectual, and even spiritual life. College faculty events are rampant with comments that reflect the insecurities of intellectual jealousy and political games. Church conventions are poisoned by those who want to see their own favorite elected to a position of power. Governmental circles, from city to national arenas, evidence deadly skills at hurling stunning blows based on half-truths or downright lies. Who cares? The object seems to be to win at all costs.

Gossip, defined as idle chatter, is all too often deadly through abuse. If you are the victim of such a destructive force, you know the pain gossip can inflict. I hope you can see clearly that in a twisted way, gossip is a sort of compliment. Obviously the subject of the gossip is important. Since much of this idle chatter is based on jealousy, that means the gossipers see in you the qualities they wish they had. They really feel inferior to you. Instead of being hurt by this type of verbal abuse, you may end up feeling very good. The effects of some abuse can be healed through this kind of knowledge.

In 1949, George Orwell wrote a frighteningly prophetic book entitled simply, *1984.* His fictional tale depicted a society that had lost its capacity to care. Bit by bit those who peopled this world drifted into a cold, mechanical society that could no longer feel or express love.

Once I believed that no human being could drift beyond the pale of redemption if someone just showed enough love. Now in the nineties—well past 1984—we must face the facts. All around us we see people who demonstrate the deadening syndrome depicted in *1984.* Before we realize what is happening, we ourselves can catch the contagion of such a sick world.

This infection can happen through verbal abuse with all its implications: the deep hurts that never heal, but are only covered with protective callouses; the instinctive need to get even to preserve some degree of personal power; the gradual growth toward competitive aggression that climbs over the toppled forms of those one can push down. This destructive force expressed through abusive words is insidious in its relentless progression.

Keep a careful watch over your own mind and emotions. Commit yourself to avoiding the callouses. Stay, or become, strongly gentle, kindly humorous, wisely nurturing, and carefully protective. And in the process of treating others in such a positive way, may you find peace and a safe haven for your own spirit!

✦ ✦ ✦

Study Questions

1. What angry encounters with harassed ticket agents, disgruntled store clerks, waitresses, or others in the world at large have you experienced as especially abusive?

2. How did you respond to such abuse? In what ways have you been tempted to retaliate and multiply the pain?

3. List any times you may have boldly (or timidly) tried to offer some correction to such abuse. What were the results?

4. In what ways have you ever felt put down as sexually or racially or otherwise inferior and assigned a subservient role in a social group? How did this make you feel and how did you respond?

5. Describe any incidents when you were the target of damaging gossip. How did you respond?

6. How might you wish you had responded? Can you learn to handle such situations in a strong and positive way?

Part Three

Forms and Effects of Verbal Abuse

TEN

Guises and Disguises

✦ ✦ ✦

O N A RECENT PLANE FLIGHT I was seated beside a delightful man. Even at the airport I had noticed his gracious
manner and kindly face. I especially enjoyed getting to
know him better in that peep-hole of intimacy peculiar to
in-flight seat mates.

During our conversation we talked about the great gift of
humor in a cold, impersonal world. A bit wistfully, he stated,
"I used to love to tell jokes, and I was pretty good at it. I
could always get people to laugh. But then I realized most
jokes made someone a victim. So I knew I'd rather give up
jokes rather than to have a laugh at someone's expense!"

What a rare and beautiful person. This man had once enjoyed poking fun at ethnic groups, until he realized the
pain his humor caused. He had decided that such humor is
cruel and willingly gave up his role as story-teller and laugh-
maker until he could find harmless jokes.

HARMFUL HUMOR

My fellow traveler had once again reiterated my own concern. Even laughter, as necessary as it is, becomes abuse

129

when it targets one of God's children. Not only is such humor aimed at national and ethnic groups, it also is common among professional antagonists. Doctors poke fun at attorneys who fling it right back. Both doctors and lawyers tell derogatory jokes about insurance agents, and they all poke fun at the clergy.

Lest I be falsely accused of being dour and rigid, incapable of humor, let me quickly counter any such ideas. I'm a strong believer in the proverb that states, "A merry heart does good like a medicine." I try in every situation to dig out some scraps of humor and use that laughter to defuse all sorts of tension and animosity.

To be healthy humor, the joke needs to focus on some universal truth that can be applied to everyone. I recently had the fun of being on a national TV program. We were discussing the topic of mothers and babies from various perspectives. One of the hosts projected a picture of herself as a tiny baby and asked her male co-host to identify it. Of course he guessed incorrectly. When she revealed that she was that baby, he was taken off guard.

In a flash, this quick-witted man recovered and asked her when she began wearing a wig—since as a baby she was bald but now has lovely hair. The laughter of the live audience grew even louder when he said, with a pat to his own hairless scalp, "We must be related."

The good humor began with her daring to risk an unrehearsed joke on public TV. The photograph, of course, was relevant to a point she was clarifying about the chosen topic. And she knew her co-host could quickly find the fun and prevent any pain to others by confidently turning it upon himself.

Being able to laugh at one's own self is a great skill, and laughing *with* someone else is fun. But laughing *at* another is likely to be abusive. Cynical wit may be aimed at one's own self, so it is each individual's choice whether or not to do that. If such humor focuses on traits or experiences most people have had, then they are also likely to consider it humorous.

Such shared laughter seems harmless—unless, of course, the person puts him/herself down because of low self-esteem. No better, and perhaps even worse, is to abuse one's self in such a manner rather than to abuse another. Insulting one's self even in humor may cause others to lose respect as well.

On a radio interview a lady called in to describe her husband's habit of putting himself down. His father had ridiculed and otherwise verbally abused him until he finally left home. The habit of feeling inadequate was so ingrained in that man that he picked up just where his dad had left off. At any small mistake, he repeatedly laughed at himself and reminded his wife of how stupid and awkward he was. She found herself struggling to build him up, but was beginning to wonder if he really was inadequate!

Rick's habit is another example of abusive humor aimed at one's own self—ridicule which is often silenced by dangerous escapades. Rick was smaller than most of his teenage peers, a physical disadvantage that pushed him to prove himself at all costs. He had grown up with a strong and powerful father. In his efforts to get his son to exercise and develop some muscles, this man teasingly called him a wimp and urged him to lift weights so he wouldn't look like such a sissy.

Over time, Rick determined that no one would ever again call him a wimp or a sissy. He began to attempt risky feats. He climbed tall trees with dead branches and teetered precariously on high limbs. He would call down to his friends below and laugh at his own daring. His bicycle became a weapon as he did dangerous tricks with it. And always, when the feat was over, Rick would laugh at his achievements.

As you can imagine, he met many failures. His was a familiar face at the emergency room of the local hospital. He had broken bones, multiple cuts, severe bruises, and occasional hospital stays. Rick was obviously accident prone. And in every case of injury, he was full of laughs. No one could call him a scaredy-cat or a sissy. Dad was wrong! And so was Rick. He acted as if proving his father wrong was his greatest joy. But he was abusing himself to the point of risking his life.

Laughing at one's own or another's calamity is often called "gallows humor"—a name out of the American frontier. Seeing an outlaw hung became a sort of free entertainment in those days. Anyone who talks in a humorous manner about serious, life and death issues is practicing a deadly sort of verbal abuse—at himself or anyone else.

To evaluate the way you use humor, here are seven questions. As you think about them, you can readily see for yourself if you verbally abuse others or yourself through humor.

1. At what type of jokes do I laugh the most?
2. What type of jokes do I remember most easily? Do I repeat them?
3. Do I cover up feelings of clumsiness or inadequacy by laughing at myself?
4. Do I label my children or friends in terms that create laughter?
5. Are my children's nicknames endearing or ridiculing?
6. When a serious or even possibly dangerous event occurs, do I tend to laugh it off?
7. When I find myself at fault or believe others are critical of me, do I cover it up with a joke?

If you can clearly answer no to these questions, you pass! You are probably not one who abuses yourself or others through humor. That's great, because you are free to enjoy healthy fun, knowing you are not inflicting pain.

Now let's explore what you may do if you grew up accustomed to such a form of abuse.

1. Be aware of it! By definition, treatment that is habitual can readily become ignored. If you now know that you

were habitually ridiculed, you have begun recovering from that sort of pain.

2. Every time you find yourself the brunt of such laughter, refuse to join in. It works best if you become serious but not angry. Explain how you feel when you are laughed at and explain to those who are doing so that you plan to leave the room whenever this happens. Then follow through, returning casually when the laughter has subsided.

3. Carefully check out your belief system about yourself. If you perceive yourself as a person worthy of ridicule, reconsider. Chances are, that perception is false. Look at your good qualities and strengths. If you do have areas of weakness, does ridicule help you grow and improve? I doubt it. Instead, develop a workable plan for correcting your mistakes and growing beyond them.

Learn from your experiences. Never again do you need to take the pain of ridicule. And, of course, avoid ever practicing it.

MANIPULATION

Randy and Mary had weathered many storms in their marriage of some twenty-five years. As time went by, they had recognized some pretty important differences in their values and priorities but had gradually learned to negotiate most of them. They were also learning to accept each other with respect in spite of their differences.

One area remained, however, in which they could find no common ground. That area revolved around Randy's handling of their finances. For years, Mary had given him free reign—except for occasional arguments about her own spending money. Then she began to feel that Randy was making some big mistakes in the family budget. Somewhat against her own values, Mary at last determined that she would manage a portion of their income in her own way, and Randy could then do as he liked with the rest.

For some time this decision worked well and Mary had saved a small amount of money, enough to make her feel secure. That security, however, was short-lived. Randy encountered some unexpectedly high bills and did not have enough money to repay them. Of course, he immediately requested that his wife come to his aid with her own funds.

When Mary demurred, Randy became angry. Knowing her intimately, he accused, "You're just another domineering female. As soon as you got control of a little money, you suddenly lost interest in the bigger picture. You know I want to leave a nice inheritance for the children someday. Without your help at this crucial point, I'm likely to lose a lot of money. But of course, you don't care about them. All you're interested in is your own little sugar bowl."

What a masterpiece of manipulation and verbal abuse! His accusations hit at the very heart of Mary's value system. She did care about the children's future. And no, she really did not want to be a domineering, controlling woman. Yes, she had tried to be supportive of her husband.

But Randy refused to be put off. With several variations on his abusive themes, he finally saw his wife crumble. Mary depleted her laboriously saved little nest egg to prove that none of the things he had said about her were true. Several times over the years, this scenario was repeated. Randy knew exactly how to manipulate Mary until she caved in to his wishes.

People use many ways, large and small, to manipulate each other. If you can identify with Mary—people-pleaser that she was—then you know the pain of manipulative abuse!

Lois and Ben loved to have their adult daughter and her husband come home every Sunday for dinner. Their daughter and her husband had many activities of their own and enjoyed a meal with Lois and Ben at times, just not *every* Sunday. Try as they would to explain their position, however, Lois refused to accept their feelings. At first, she simply became more insistent. Reluctantly, they dutifully came to dinner but left as quickly as possible.

Gradually, Lois resorted to other means. She suffered from arthritis and truly was uncomfortable at times. But she began to emphasize her pain. She limped a little and complained of the stiffness in her hands. Couldn't her daughter just help her with opening food containers? She really needed her at least once a week.

When her daughter and son-in-law saw her out for a brisk walk one Wednesday, they began to see through her scheme. They put up even more resistance to this unhappy ritual. Lois then began to telephone her daughter and detail her ailments at length, insinuating that she might not live too much longer. Such a threat was difficult to debate. Lois was growing older and the ailments of the elderly are likely to be more serious than one wants to believe. Perhaps they were misjudging Lois.

And so they kept going for Sunday dinners, doubtful about Lois' honesty and resentful of this duty. A business move finally resolved the problem. Lois' son-in-law was transferred to a distant state. Their move finally ended the debate—no more unhappy Sunday dinners. Now over ten years since that move, Lois and Ben are still going for walks—although admittedly a little slower. And their daughter and son-in-law's absence has not been the death of her. When they do visit, they have a wonderful time, but they have at last been allowed to leave home. Both physically and emotionally, everyone in that family is free.

Even Lois now realizes that some of her unbending insistence was related to her own parents' rituals. She finally remembered that, as newlyweds, she and Ben used to hate those Sunday meals. And she discovered the relief of freedom from the work those special meals demanded.

How sad that Lois abused her family by making them feel

sorry for her and even guilty for her imagined neglect. Be careful to avoid perpetrating such abuse. And if you are the victim, do not give in to it. Check out the truth and do not let yourself be manipulated against your better judgment.

A psychiatrist mentor of mine once taught me a classic truth: *what's good for anyone in a given situation has to be good for everyone.* The corollary is obvious: if something is not good for everyone involved, it simply cannot be good for any one individual. Verbal abuse, even in the sometimes subtle form of manipulation, is a bad practice.

In the art of manipulation, you may have perceived several steps, each progressively more intense. Randy started to manipulate Mary through a simple statement of need. When she failed to respond, he progressed to a clear, forceful request. When she continued to hesitate, he actually "bullied" her verbally. With derogatory statements and implications that were barely true, he led her to give in to his demands by appealing to her most cherished values.

The same progression is apparent with Lois. Their family dinners began with the expectations left over from her youth. They went on to specific, weekly invitations that were forcefully stated. The next step was to induce their sympathy for her failing health, which finally developed into the threat that she would soon die. Then they would be sorry for not having spent time with her.

The basis for deciding whether or not manipulation is abusive rests in these steps, and the seeming helplessness of the victim to counteract them. Whether or not the manipulation succeeds depends on some degree of co-dependency on the part of the target. Mary had grown up feeling responsible for her parents' happiness. If she failed to please them, they made her feel guilty and generally miserable. It was largely to avoid such verbal abuse from those parents that Mary learned how to be a people-pleaser, even when she knew better in her mind. Mary's personal happiness depended on keeping others happy—which, I believe, is the core of co-dependency.

Whenever abuse becomes habitual and crippling, some degree of co-dependency is involved. But much has been written about that. You need primarily to recognize your own role in the dynamics of your particular situation. You can learn that your inner joy and peace are not dependent on the happiness of others, but are gifts from God to be accepted, enjoyed, and taught to others. Because of loyalties and commitments, however, the target of manipulation often feels he or she must give in.

But remember my friend's statement. If giving in is not right or good for you, it cannot be good for the manipulator either. You are not being counter-abusive if you gently and clearly establish your own limits. What can you give in time, energy, or money without resenting it? Can you give that much gladly, even if there is little expression of gratitude? What if your manipulator becomes angry and rejects you? Can you stay friendly and avoid retaliation? If so, you can join the ranks of emotionally healthy, non-abusive people!

A CRITICAL SPIRIT

"Gwen, you didn't even dust that table at all. You've spent all morning dusting two rooms and as usual, you've half done the job. I can see dust everywhere I look. You're just a careless, lazy girl. If you'd get your mind off selfishly reading your books, you could concentrate on some worthwhile accomplishments!"

Mother's voice increased in both scale and intensity as she repeated the usual Saturday morning lecture once again. Gwen had vowed when she got up that day that she would finally do her dusting job exactly right. Her mother would not be able to find even a speck of dust when she inspected the job.

Anxious to please, Gwen meticulously rubbed the well-oiled dust cloth over every corner and surface of every piece of furniture, just as she had every Saturday as long as she could remember. And each new weekend, Gwen renewed her vow—this time, perfect. Yet it never was. It wasn't even good, let alone perfect.

Those harsh negative words still echo in Gwen's adult head at times. "Careless, lazy, selfish." These hopeless words of ugliness often tempted her to just give up. Why she never did is not easy to explain. Perhaps the approval of others finally outweighed her mother's criticalness. Maybe, underneath her disappointment at Mom's disapproval, was some good common sense whereby she just knew her mother was somehow unfair in her judgments.

At any rate, Gwen survived, and not long after, she informed me she was doing well. Here's how she knew! One day she was busy in her own home carefully dusting the coffee table. The dark wood gleamed until it almost reflected her face. Gwen suddenly grew a bit pensive as she remembered those long ago Saturdays. With a glow of pride, she thought, "What a shame Mother never knew what a champion duster I am!"

We have already discussed the damage of verbal abuse to children, and Gwen's story reiterates that sad fact. So be very sure you are not too critical of your children. Your best efforts to help them improve and grow in excellence will come not from harsh criticism but from encouragement.

Stan was a scholarly man, well-known in his own profession, exceedingly conscientious, a true perfectionist. The trouble was, Stan also expected everyone else to be perfect as well. In time he was appointed to the search committee for a new pastor in his church. Of course, this demanding perfectionist knew exactly what specifications were necessary for the one the group should select.

The trouble was, no such person existed in real life—only in Stan's fantasies. The committee contended with his stubborn refusal of every candidate they found. His dour looks and critical comments raised enough doubts to defeat vote after vote of the other members. At last, in desperation, a minister was found whom Stan could reluctantly tolerate. The man moved, settled in to the new congregation, and quickly became loved and respected by everyone—everyone except Stan, of course. Every time a sermon was given, Stan took notes. He diligently checked the sermon content against his own personal beliefs. When he discovered a difference, Stan soon found an opportunity to tell the hard-working clergyman where he was in error.

Stan did not remember to commend the good things the pastor did. He had no comments when even he could find no real faults with the sermon. Only the critical statements were worth bringing up, Stan seemed to believe.

The clergyman tried ever so hard to be thorough in his studies and careful in his statements. But inevitably, there was Stan, waiting until the congregants had left so that he could challenge the pastor, week after week. That clergyman struggled mightily to find comfort in the comments of others, but the criticism of this determined man seemed to outweigh them all. He was emotionally bruised and scarred by the constant barrage of verbal abuse.

Marriages are often marred by such chronic criticalness. One is too heavy or too thin, too fastidious or too careless, too stingy or too much a spendthrift. He likes to go out with the fellows; she clings too much.

The judgments people make are usually based on the families from which they came. The conflicts with parents that were never fully resolved are repeated with the spouse, often with redoubled vigor. Surely, this time it will all come out right, the wife believes—her husband will change for her sake. Or the husband believes he can make his wife different—more to his liking.

It is from such deeply buried but intense needs that the harsh criticisms of marriages grow. Rarely does a husband intend to abuse his wife, or vice versa. But abuse follows the crying needs of a person's innermost being—a desperate attempt to diminish their own emotional pain, at all costs.

If you understand this truth, you will see how essential it

is that individuals become whole, secure, and mature before marriage. When each spouse has his or her own sense of well-being, worth, love, and peace, then marriage will enhance those qualities. Without that inner core of health in each individual, the marriage will travel a rocky road.

Many studies of school children have shown that they worsen in academic skills when harsh attitudes are displayed by teachers. On the other hand, when praise and encouragement are practiced, even resistant children try harder and do better. One popular trend is to put the names of children who misbehave on the blackboard. Since misbehavior is usually the expression of poor self-esteem, it is difficult to see how such punitive measures can help.

By openly criticizing children who already feel inept and stupid, their poor self-images are only reinforced. When children lack a healthy sense of worth, help is much more possible by identifying an area of good ability and helping them to demonstrate that strength.

One exceptional teacher had put great energy into this search for something positive in every one of her students. One boy challenged her to an extreme extent! But at last she found the answer to helping him. Max loved tiny cars and would bring several in his pockets almost daily. Unfortunately, he would play with them instead of studying. After confiscating numbers of them and trying vainly to get this child to pay attention to his school work, his teacher stumbled onto a solution.

The class had a show and tell time, so she helped this lad learn all about "Matchbox Cars." One day Max gave a truly fascinating talk on this subject to the class. They were all amazed at his depth of knowledge. The teacher then found some books on cars and assigned a report to him. Again, this homework struck a responsive chord. As Max discovered that others valued his interests, he began to feel important. When his reading assignments focused on his special interest, school work was no longer drudgery. This teacher knew that harshness and criticism had never helped this silently resistant lad. By entering his world of tiny cars and showing him they had value, she had helped him discover his own worth.

As you read these examples of the abusive impact of criticalness, you may have been able to see yourself in similar situations. If so, you could perhaps feel once again the sadness, anger, and rebelliousness of long ago. It is very likely that you have more recent examples, as well, in which you have endured critical abuse from family or people at work.

I can guarantee that you will continue to experience such treatment because the world we live in is a harsh one. But I can also offer you great hope! By learning to understand, you can forgive; and through total forgiveness, you can come to know healing. Once you discover your own worth and have released old resentments and fears, your future growth can be limitless. We'll deal with that process in the last section.

✦ ✦ ✦

Study Questions

1. Describe times when you have felt victimized by someone else's cruel humor. How did you react or respond?

2. In what ways do you tend to put yourself down through the use of abusive humor? How do you see such a pattern as a reflection of low self-esteem?

3. In what ways do you perceive yourself as worthy of ridicule or laughter?

4. What specific incidents can you recall when someone manipulated you through verbal abuse to achieve their own purposes? Did you feel helpless to counteract such abuse?

5. Describe specific incidents when you have experienced harsh and abusive words from a perfectionist or overly critical person. How did such remarks make you feel?

6. How can you begin to gently and clearly establish your own limits even in the face of anger, criticism, or rejection? How can you move from painful feelings to positive actions?

ELEVEN

The Name Game

✦ ✦ ✦

WE HAVE ALREADY DISCUSSED THE ABUSE of labeling children. All children possess certain traits and habits—those inherited from their parents and others influenced and shaped by their environment. These individual characteristics need to be recognized simply as that—not as fatal flaws.

But because of their parents' values, attitudes, and habits, children interpret these traits as either bad or good. When parents perceive a certain quality as negative, they are very likely to attach that derogatory label to the child. Some examples which I have already used include words like shy, stupid, awkward, selfish, careless, or worse. If you were verbally abused, you may recall your own labels.

As an adult, you can now understand that you didn't originally deserve that label. Your family, through their mistaken perceptions, laid it on you. You may very well have learned to live up to that derogatory description, so that your own memories deceptively make you believe you had earned it. Reconsider that assumption as interpreted in the light of these insights into the nature of verbal abuse. Try to view yourself in a completely different way, instead of holding to the old childhood perception!

If only they would stop to think, parents could use totally different terms to describe the developing traits of their children, especially early on. Instead of a shy or bashful child, what if a parent saw a reserved and cautious one? Instead of being stupid, a child may be curious—more eager to explore than to memorize and parrot answers. Rather then awkward or clumsy, one might at least say "learning" or "unpracticed." Selfishness might be seen as a child's valuing their belongings or saving materials. Carelessness might be the beginning of a set of values that simply are not materially centered but person-centered.

Abusive labels are almost always distortions or misperceptions of ordinary or sometimes even wonderful traits. How one sees and interprets them, in the light of past experiences, deems them as good or bad. All too commonly, children learn to live up to their labels. See to it, as much as you can, that the labels you give your children are positive ones!

DESIGNER LABELS

Children are not the only ones who are labeled. Much racism could be eliminated if we would stop talking about minorities, blacks or African Americans, Asians, Hispanics, Indians or native Americans. While these terms are by no means abusive in the minds of most of us, wouldn't it promote integration if we knew all people as simply human beings?

I myself am a "senior citizen" and have been for several years. I work hard to convince myself of that, however, by telling folks I am sixty-five years old. I feel so well that I can hardly believe I have really reached that age! Actually, I can see some nice advantages to growing older. But in the minds of many, if not most Westerners, *old is bad*—implying weakness, dependency, mental senility, and uselessness. Do those terms sound like verbal abuse? They certainly do to me. I like to believe I still have a lot to offer my small world. And so do most senior citizens.

Another label that tragically has become abusive is this: he or she is such a "religious" person. All too often such a term sets a person apart into a strange and mystical category that seems a bit frightening. Religion, despite some growth in church attendance, is no longer a very respected entity in today's Western society.

A person of great depth and high moral values can be neutralized, or even entirely negated, by such a neat label. And when we get into sub-group labels, an even greater danger of abusiveness emerges. If people practice a conservative theology, either Jewish or Christian, they are at risk of being called fanatics or fundamentalists. Never mind whether or not such individuals are trying to be honest and conscientious. Their efforts can be quickly and effectively discounted by such demeaning labels.

A mother who sacrifices to stay at home to raise her children may be cast aside by her career-oriented sisters, simply by labeling her "over-protective" and "lazy." And a woman who has to go to work, for whatever the reason, can be equally put down by stay-at-home moms. They may label her "ambitious" or "selfish."

A conscientious person who works a bit past stopping time at work is often labeled an "apple polisher" (or worse). Such people are often shunned by those with opposing values who call them "clock watchers" or "ne'er-do-wells" (or worse!). In the teacher's lounge, a person who sticks to the task and refuses to join in the gossip sessions can be labeled a "principal's pet," "a snob," or a "know-it-all." Those who spend their time indulging in idle talk are easily seen by their co-workers as "gossips" and "back stabbers."

On and on it goes! You need only take the time to observe and listen to notice this process in action. You can fill a notebook with labels that are clearly words that hurt. Once you become aware, you need to decide whether you are guilty of similar practices. If so, break the habit! It feels so good to learn to see others as okay as yourself!

If you yourself are a person who accepts labels, let me suggest a new idea. Rather than submit to derogatory labels, re-fuse to do so. One method for stopping others from contin-uing to title you is to confront them. The very next time you hear yourself called a name you find obnoxious, be pre-pared. Find your own ideas and words, but I suggest some-thing like this:

"Tim, you're my brother and you've known me a long time. And you've always called me 'Skinny.' When you call me that, I feel really sad because it implies that I'm ugly and undesirable. Let me tell you that's not true! I happen to be slender and healthy. Would you be please call me by my real name from now on? Cindi is a name I love and I'd really like you to use it. Okay?"

You may not have realized that you harbor resentment about an ugly nickname. Furthermore, you may not have considered the fact that you have both the right and the power to stop the use of abusive labels. I can hear many of you making excuses for your "labelers." You may have convinced yourself that it's just a pet name, a sign of being special.

Certainly many nicknames are endearing and may reflect that rich intimacy families need to experience. If your label is not of that caliber, however, stop responding to it after you have explained your feelings. If you do this in a firm and kindly manner, your request is not likely to prompt ill will. You have more power than you've realized!

SCREAMING EPITHETS

A few years ago, a teacher friend of mine named Pat Holt learned from a number of her students how abusive scream-ing can be. In preparation for a Mother's Day event, she wanted to know what her pupils liked best about their moms and what troubled them the most. Pat discovered many qual-ities they liked—perhaps her nice smelling perfume, her pretty hair, or her reading or playing with them.

But almost all of the children revealed that their biggest concern about their mothers was their screaming. To these children, it was not just the words but the loud voice and the intense anger that scared or worried them. Some of them recognized that their mothers' screaming made them angry enough to scream back. Pat and I wrote a book about the problem of habitually screaming mothers. (*When You Feel Like Screaming*. Holt, Pat, & Ketterman, Grace, Harold Shaw, Wheaton, Il., 1988.)

Almost all children experience screaming as verbal abuse, sometimes even more painful than physical abuse. Are you a screaming mom? Perhaps your mother yelled. Maybe you carry an unbearable load of stress and scream whenever you hit your breaking point. Maybe you've learned that yelling works to get your child to hear and obey you.

Whatever the reason, screaming doesn't work in the long run. Except for a few emergency situations, parental yelling is verbal abuse. And it will prove to be effective, as will physical abuse, only until your child learns to do it back as expertly as you have modeled. There are better ways to accomplish your purposes.

A great many screaming mothers find that their mothers yelled at them. Perhaps you are one of those people who grew up with a screaming mom! Like the children in our study, you learned to scream back at your mom. And now you use that method of correction on your own children. The mothers I know who do so nearly always hate their habit and feel guilty about it—yet seem powerless to stop themselves. What a predicament!

If you are among that large group of people, you will be interested in learning how to stop. In Chapter 16, you will see how the Twelve Steps of Alcoholics Anonymous apply to you. You, too, can not only overcome your hurts but also stop hurting others!

Screaming, like labeling, is not limited to parents. Siblings scream at each other and at parents. Playmates and classmates often yell out their frustrations at each other. At school, at work, in snarled traffic and public events, people scream out their pent up rage. Yelling at someone makes a person *feel* so powerful. But it is almost always a sign of inner insecurity, a sort of bullying by grownups and children alike that results in embarrassment, pain, and mistrust.

It is important to differentiate loud talking from screaming. On a trip with a tour group, I found myself intimidated by a man who talked so loudly that I assumed he must be angry. As days went by, however, I learned he was one of the most compassionate persons in the group. He just spoke loudly. He was part of a family who expressed themselves freely and it was just their way to speak in loud voices. But when the yelling is based on anger and statements are made that attack and hurt others, then it is abuse.

ABUSIVE BODY LANGUAGE

Body language can also become a type of abuse. If you disagree, let me remind you of a commonly used cliché: "If looks could kill, she'd have been dead." Have any of us escaped such scathing looks? In fact, few of us can claim that we have never sent one!

Not long ago I patiently waited for a parking place in a busy parking area. The pavement was slick with freezing rain, so I wanted to park close to the store. Just as the car on which I was waiting backed out, a sleek sports car adroitly turned into the vacant spot. The driver barely missed my front fender. What a brash, rude young "jerk," I thought. I glared at him, and when I encountered him in the aisles of the store, I glared again. I suspect he was too calloused to be aware of my withering stare, but it made me feel better! You see, I personally experienced the temporary pleasure of getting even, in a tiny measure, by my angry look. The problem is, of course, my behavior didn't really help him or me!

A look of disgust, disdain, or outright rage is clearly readable. Studies show us that such facial expressions are universal and identical in all parts of the world. Such body language shares in common our recurring definition of verbal abuse: *it puts down another person, hurts feelings, and inflicts pain that results in emotional scars.*

In my profession, I have become expert in reading faces, postures, and gestures. Words and tone of voice may readily be trained to deceive the listener. And a superficial smile may temporarily mask the real feelings underneath. But over time, inner, habitual emotions etch their tell-tale lines into the faces of their owners.

People whose body language is abusive develop a parallel attitude that repels others. The down-turned mouth, set jaw, tight lips, and furrowed brow of an angry, abusive person send a clear message: "I may hurt you. Stay away!"

What sort of person do you want to be? What does your face reveal about you? Do you like what you see in the mirror? If not, take a look at your inner attitudes and feelings. It's never too late to change. First, work on your inner being, and then begin to smile instead of frown, to look kindly rather than to snarl, and to relax those frowns into gentleness. In Chapter 14, we will explore some ways you can tell if you have become an abuser.

UNFAVORABLE COMPARISONS

Steve's first wife had died after thirty years of marriage, throughout which they shared many episodes of disagreement and even major fights. Roberta died after a somewhat lengthy illness. During that time, the two of them had grown especially close. Steve was devoted to her and most of those earlier struggles had receded in his memory.

As so commonly happens, Steve idealized his departed wife and genuinely grieved over his loss. But in only a few months he met a new lady friend and in due time they were married. Shirley had never married before, and the romance and fun of their honeymoon were a daily thrill for her.

And then they went home—to *Steve's* house, filled with memories and material things that did not belong to the new wife. Photographs of Roberta and Steve were scattered about the house. Shirley understood that Steve would have some grieving to finish and was wise enough to know that he needed to be the one to remove these old mementos. But once in a while she would see him look with longing at Roberta's pictures or avoid her eyes when an old favorite song was played. While Shirley yearned to comfort him, she felt awkward and uncertain about what to do or say.

To help Steve through his moods, his new wife tried to plan special events. Shirley especially loved to cook and entertain, so she planned cozy, intimate dinners with a few special friends. The very first time she did this kind of entertaining almost became the last. From the appetizer to the dessert—including the table setting and centerpiece—Steve found fault.

"Roberta never served tomato soup with roast lamb," he complained. And, "Roberta always had a low bowl of flowers on the table. Your centerpiece is too tall." And, "Roberta never did think the Smiths and Joneses would be good company for each other. Are you sure you should have invited both couples?" By the time the guests arrived, Shirley was nearly in tears and the tension was palpable.

Fortunately, the newlyweds could confront each other and Shirley certainly needed to do so. She explained that she was *not* Roberta and described how Steve's comparisons had hurt her. While making some allowance for his grieving process, Shirley made it quite clear that she would be doing things the best she could. She would certainly try to please her husband in every possible way. And then Shirley clearly requested, "Steve, please don't ever compare me with Roberta again. I will not allow her memory to come between us. So let me comfort you until your grief is gone, and then let's build a new life together."

What a wise wife! She understood the problem, allowed for Steve's lack of sensitivity, but also stated her own position. Shirley refused to accept the abuse of her husband's unfavorable comparisons. And, thankfully, Steve could finally see the pain he had inflicted.

Consider the way Shirley dealt with this situation. She could have become hurt by this verbal abuse and silently retreated, thereby creating a major rift in her new marriage. His words actually were cruel and had hurt her deeply. But Shirley knew how to confront him in love. She showed him how she felt, explained why she felt those emotions, and clearly asked for a well-defined change. Steve, who did love her, could understand and respond without further arguing. Go and do likewise!

Such a happy ending is not always the case. We have already described the girl whose sister rated higher on her mother's value scale. And remember the son who overheard his mother state a preference for his brother as her favorite son? Such comparisons are all too common and are often stated casually, without any intention or even knowledge of the pain they create. But in the silent heart of the unfavored child, the wounds are deep and the scars are permanent.

My sister taught school for many years. I saw how hard she worked, trying to teach her young students all they needed to know. She was necessarily strict and brooked no nonsense. While her pupils would later thank her for her dedication, they didn't always like her methods at the time. Early in every school year, my sister would often come home in tears. She was so weary of hearing, "Well, I don't like doing three papers of arithmetic! Mrs. Harris only made us do one!" Or, "You make us work all the time! Mr. James let us play games sometimes!"

Whether or not these other teachers had really been so easy became irrelevant. The students, even in elementary school, had mastered the craft of verbal abuse. As a conscientious teacher, my sister was not as loved or accepted as the others. Yet, she wanted the best for her students and worked harder than almost any other faculty member to make that happen. She cared enough to take their abuse, because she well knew, in the long run, what was best for them!

Similar negative comparisons take place in politics, churches, jobs, and professions of all types. The basic dynamics are identical. You need to know how to cope with such abuse and to be exceedingly careful to avoid practicing it. Be sure to find within yourself all the good that is there, concentrating your efforts on enjoying and developing those strengths. Improve your weaknesses the most you can, but compare yourself only with *your* best—not another's.

Once you have mastered the art of self-acceptance, you will be less vulnerable to others' unfavorable comparisons. And you will be better able to avoid ever hurting someone else by that process. In the next chapter, we will further consider the importance of self-esteem in this whole equation of giving and receiving verbal abuse.

✦ ✦ ✦

Study Questions

1. List specific negative labels applied to you as a child. What kind of feelings do you still harbor about an ugly nickname? Do you now see that such labels were the result of mistaken perceptions and that you did not originally deserve them?

2. Have you ever been stung by some racist, sexist, or other kind of categorizing remark or label? If so, describe the incidents. How did you respond?

3. In what ways are you a person who readily accepts labels? How could you respond differently or confront the labeler? Do you impulsively label others at times?

4. Are you a screaming parent? Did your parents scream at you? What results from parental screaming do you see in your own family? What do you think may lie behind screaming, e.g., inner insecurity, fears, anxiety, frustrations?

TWELVE

Permanent Scars

◆ ◆ ◆

THROUGHOUT THIS BOOK, you have learned that verbal abuse is not just momentary but often *lifelong* in its impact and even *life-shaping* through its influence. Let's examine some of these permanent effects.

Many studies have been conducted and books written about the importance of self-esteem in both the development and functioning of human beings. Every adult who works with children is likely to agree with the importance of this primary ingredient of an emotionally healthy person.

What many adults fail to realize is the need for consistently positive feedback to a child in order to build self-esteem. Even less do they stop to think about the almost irreparable damage of hurtful, negative comments to a child. Their intention is to correct and mold children into gleaming reflections of themselves, and finally into successful adults.

The foundations of verbal abuse are laid in childhood. Parents who verbally abuse their children were almost always treated in this fashion when they themselves were young. And their children, accustomed to painful words from their earliest memory, are more than likely to carry on the practice—first with themselves, then with friends and siblings, and ultimately with their own children.

As such practices continue, they inevitably invade our entire culture. In my work as a psychiatrist, I frequently encounter depressed people. And I find them to be people who are, in a sense, addicted or habituated to profoundly negative thoughts. "I am not worthy to live." "I'm no good." "I'll never make it." "I was a mistake, an accident; even my mother didn't really want me." "Only death can release me from such misery." "I'm an imposter—I can't really do this job. I'm only fooling people. The only thing I'm good at is failure."

You have undoubtedly heard and perhaps stated some form of these negative, self-abusive comments at some point in your own life. Have you ever considered how these negative thoughts influence your attitudes and behavior? You may not have thought about the subtle permission they give you to fail. In fact, more than a permission, you may unwittingly experience them more as a command. A failure is what I'm *supposed* to be! I'll obediently fail!

If you can destroy your own self-esteem, based on those shaky foundations, you can also find out how to stop doing that and learn to build a positive self-image. We'll work on that later. That takes time. At this point, let's explore some practical ingredients of self-esteem.

DAMAGE TO SELF-ESTEEM

Entire volumes have been written on building self-esteem. In this book, I do not have enough space to even summarize the research that has been done on this important topic. Here is a helpful list, however, of a few of the ways in which self-esteem can be built.

1. Unconditional acceptance is the very cornerstone of self-esteem. A quote I learned many years ago was attributed to Alfred Adler, an early psychiatrist. "It is in love and through love, either human or divine, that one learns to accept himself—because another accepts him first."

Biblical truth states this vital fact much more simply: "We

love, because [God] first loved us" (1 Jn 4:19). Knowing we are loved is powerful evidence that we possess personal worth. The fact that we are cherished means that we are valuable. Look for those who love you, just like you are. Perhaps you can only think of God. That is enough to enable you to begin to love yourself. When you make this commitment, self-esteem becomes planted within you!

2. Approval is another ingredient of self-esteem. As a child, you didn't know whether or not your efforts and projects were worth anything. You were entirely dependent on the opinions and verdicts of others. Perhaps you lived in an environment that was more critical than approving. If so, you were indeed a victim of verbal abuse which made it difficult for you to build that vital sense of worth.

But now, as an adult, you may reconsider the past. Try to remember times when you knew, even as a child, that you were really good and that things you did were commendable—even without the benefit of recognition and praise at that time. In remembering, try to capture a bit of the glow of your success. Use those memories to cultivate your knowledge of personal worth.

3. One of the major spoilers of self-esteem is guilt. All of us feel guilty at times for truly wrong behavior or even for imagined misdeeds. If you are guilty of hurting yourself or others or of hurting the heart of God in any way, you can be forgiven. To enjoy forgiveness, you have only to follow these steps:

a. Admit that you have done wrong.
b. Commit firmly to change so you do not repeat that wrong.
c. Make as right as possible the wrong you did.
d. Accept God's promises to forgive you.
e. Forgive yourself and put it all behind you.

If you *feel* guilty for not being perfect, or as good as you feel you should be, you need information. That information includes:

    a. Your honest assessment regarding your very best efforts. I suspect you did the best you knew how most of the time.

    b. A fair evaluation of the expectations others placed on you. Much guilt is fostered on people through unrealistic demands of others. If that is true for you, you can let go of such unfairness. You and God are now in charge. God will be fair to you. Will you?

    c. Set your goals fairly now. You need no longer live under impossible standards. Continue to stretch yourself and grow, but no longer do you need to habitually fail because others will not allow you to succeed. Rid yourself of false guilt. Work through the steps of healing for real guilt. You will then be well on your way to experiencing self-esteem.

4. Self-esteem grows from successes. The more risks you take, the greater is the likelihood that you will experience successes. If you know you are really good at even one thing, you are going to experience improvement in most other areas of your life. A study proved this correlation some years ago. Try it! Focus on small goals at first. When you are as good at those as you can get, then try other, harder goals. Learn to revel in your own sense of accomplishment rather than seeking too much reassurance from others.

5. Develop your inner values that are positive and loving. Rather than fearing someone may not like you, focus on how you can show another person that you care about him or her. Again, become more inner-directed than other-oriented in your assessments and values, either of yourself or others. By this I mean, worry only about how much you show love to others instead of how much others love you.

6. Make yourself as externally attractive as you reasonably can. If you are a woman, be sure that your hairstyle becomes you and that your makeup is appropriate. Without undue extravagance, dress in a style that suits you. Men as well as women can concentrate on staying healthy and practicing good hygiene. Then forget your appearance and pour your love and energy into making each day fulfilling and productive.

7. Remember above all, God loves you! This truth is the foundation of any feelings of self-worth. You will find many more ingredients in self-esteem as you think about it and read further. But these will get you started if you practice them faithfully.

In Part IV, we'll go into precise detail about how to get free from the damage of old verbal abuse. But today, this minute, you must make a definite decision. It takes a firm commitment if you are to make any changes. And it takes continual awareness of your old habits, sensitivity to those around you, and patient adherence to your plan, in order to win over your old practices. You, too, can develop self-esteem!

REACTION SPECTRUM

Words that hurt are exactly that—hurtful. But human beings are equipped with the instinct to avoid pain, so we develop a variety of mental and emotional mechanisms to ease the pain. With the passing of time, we may become so accustomed to both the abuse and our own defenses against it that we are hardly aware of the abuse. But from time to time, the old pain surfaces and the resentment against our abuser explodes in anguish.

On the other end of the reaction spectrum, we may turn the pain outward and aim it at others. It feels worlds better and more powerful to react in this way rather than to continue in our own anguish. We may eventually become abusers ourselves.

Between these two extremes is the most common of all responses to verbal abuse: the slow but inexorable accumulation of resentment toward the abuser. Eventually the inaccuracy and unfairness of repeatedly cruel words comes to the forefront. The victim may build a defense against further hurts through being angry.

Such anger may be a small, trickling stream that slowly erodes relationships. But it often grows into a raging torrent that may even result in destruction. Newspaper headlines all too commonly scream of murders that seem to be the tragic culmination of such stored-up resentments.

Not only are these angry feelings aimed at the abuser but they often encompass innocent bystanders. This is especially true of siblings who are perceived to be family favorites. It may well be true of other students who are less frequently criticized. And this anger certainly extends to co-workers who receive the promotions instead of the put-downs. We may be tempted to use our resentments to sabotage our boss or fellow workers.

Jerry reacted in this way. He hated having a woman supervisor. She was, admittedly, abrupt and took no nonsense. Jerry felt she did not respect him, so he would not respect her. In fact, he would make her life as difficult as he could. And Jerry did exactly that. He turned other workers against her and found many clever ways to decrease work output and quality. His own performance was just good enough that he couldn't be fired. Certainly, everyone lost in this case because of this employee's resentment over even perceived abuse in his work place.

The responses to verbal abuse may be just as destructive as the original statements were. If you are tempted to get even for any abuse you experience, think again. At the moment you will feel powerful, perhaps even gleeful to have done "one better." But think ahead. What kind of person will you be ten years from now? Do you really want to become like this abusive person you resent so much?

Allowing resentment to penetrate your soul and breed bitterness is not the best answer to abuse. It does protect you to a degree from further hurts. If you can stay angry at those who verbally abuse you, you destroy most of the power of an abuser. That person can no longer hurt you because you no longer care about him or her. But the damage this attitude does to your own emotional health and spiritual well-being can be even more crippling than abuse. You can handle your problems in a much better way.

LIMITING YOUR POTENTIAL

Do you remember the two girls in the introduction? Beth's mother basically told her she was not as intelligent as her sister. She would not be able to excel in academics, but would have to earn a living with her hands. And, in fact that's exactly what she did. The tragedy is that she was equally as bright as her sister. Beth could have continued in school and excelled in many areas. The trouble was, no one ever told her so. She felt limited in her potential and left with but one option. Beth carried her career to its peak, but was not able to break the superimposed barrier of her mother's powerful early message.

A football player's father condemned him with, "Son, you'll just never make it at football!" And he never did. Furthermore, his dad's prophecy of failure carried over into several other careers he tried. He was not successful at anything much, as long as I knew him. And he certainly tried hard! His father's words became an endless echo in his heart—"Son, you'll never make it!"

A high school student whose father predicted his total failure is already well on his way. He has come to believe that success is not worth striving for. It's safer, he feels, to stop trying, than to try really hard and face the facts of Dad's predictions coming true. If you give up all efforts, you can at least keep half-believing that you could have—if only!

You may have spent a great deal of time living down to your verbal abuser's predictions. And you could, of course, even spend the rest of your life as a loser—losing at least the degree of joy and success of which you are capable.

Or you could decide to change your course. Taking the

risks of making such a change will demand incredible courage. You may need a great deal of help, but it will be worth every bit of your investment of courage, time, energy, and money. You can still realize your capabilities and live up to them.

Let me offer some ideas I have learned about this area of living up to your potential. I have known people, young and old, who have found that these approaches are fruitful when diligently applied.

1. Psychologically, step outside of yourself and look at you. Evaluate your assets: perhaps good health, at least average good looks, a sensitive heart, some work you're good at, an interest you've never explored or developed, a mind as good as anybody's—or even better. Ask a trusted friend or relative to help you list your abilities and choose to believe their input.

2. Seek an available junior college or a vocational guidance center and ask them to give you an aptitude test. This is a fun sort of examination that will help you learn what you're good at. They can also put you in touch with resources that can enable you to get training for a new career or other creative expressions that will enrich your life.

3. Be prepared to make some sacrifices of time, freedom, and finances. Any worthwhile goal demands you give up some ease and pleasure now for future good. It's not easy, but living below your capabilities is degrading! You deserve your best!

A good friend of mine has worked for eight years at a job far below her potential. I have repeatedly encouraged her to use her truly fine mind for a better job, but Colleen has steadfastly refused to take the first step. Recently she recalled that her mother and older brother repeatedly labeled her as "lazy."

As she transferred that old concept into her current situation, she realized what had happened. Colleen is now the one who believes she is lazy. She is hesitant to risk acquiring the training that might demand harder work from her. What if her laziness bars her from success in a new area? Colleen had been choosing to play it safe rather than take the risk of failure.

4. If you are beset by fears, find someone who will encourage you. Tell that person you need tough love to jar you out of your rut of fear and help you get going toward success. And then courageously accept the help.

5. Stick by your efforts until you get the first taste of success. It will be so delightful, you'll see it's going to be great to enjoy the full meal! In the process of gaining the first glimpse of your true potential, you will be making great headway toward the healing of your old emotional abuse!

ABUSIVE WORDS CAN BECOME REALITY

A number of years ago a physician friend taught me a very important lesson: a great many decisions and actions (including verbal abuse) begin with a need. The need prompts a wish, one that if fulfilled, promises to take care of the need. The wish commonly turns into a fantasy in which the imagination sees the desire coming true. It is not difficult to see how that fantasy can, in turn, be translated into the actions that initiated this whole cycle and then lock it in.

Through a similar process, people come to believe they *are* what the words of abuse portray them to be. Remember the adolescent in Chapter 3 whose stepfather repeatedly told her she was a whore? Eileen soon began to notice prostitutes on TV and on the streets of the city where she lived. She felt angry at her stepfather and instinctively decided to hurt him as he had wounded her.

Her imagination began to work, overtime perhaps, as Eileen fantasized about becoming something like her stepfather had called her. That would certainly get even with him. She would show him. He had called her the name. She would play his game. Eileen became sexually promiscuous. She was one of the fortunate girls who became pregnant. Through the loving counsel at the maternity home she entered, this young woman turned her life around. She knew there was a better way. And she found it!

Many other persons never have this opportunity of a life-changing crisis and unfortunately continue on in the repeated patterns that recycle abuse. This recycling process results in individuals abusing themselves. Let me remind you that a great many people give themselves labels that are carbon copies of their families' labels.

For example, an abused daughter often chooses an abusive spouse. It has been said that we choose for a spouse someone like one of our parents. The trouble is, most of us have some old, unresolved conflicts with our parents. So guess what! We select that person who will re-enact those old conflicts.

At first we don't see that this dynamic is true. The person we choose for a spouse just feels comfortable—with the comfort inherent in familiarity. Time spent with that person feels vaguely like old times. And we rationalize that the negative facets of those old times will not exist in this new relationship.

But all too often they do. Remember Sarah and her discarded rosary? Her high school sweetheart turned out to be like the abusive father with which she had grown up. At first, he always acted, dressed, and appeared at his best. But when the honeymoon was over, the mask and costume came off, and Sarah was in a worse predicament than ever. Her religious convictions further locked her into a vicious marriage, in a way that her duty to her father had never done. Sarah felt forced to temporarily sacrifice her faith for her freedom.

When you understand the effects of verbal abuse, you can almost see on your own how people become abusive. But that's our next topic. How could your children or spouse be influenced to become abusers? Could you yourself be a link in the imprisoning chain of verbal abuse?

✦ ✦ ✦

Study Questions

1. What kinds of lifelong and life-shaping impact has verbal abuse had on your life? Low self-esteem? Depression? Addictions?

2. What kinds of negative or self-abusive thoughts and comments do you tend to use? How have they influenced your attitudes and behaviors?

3. List any instances of success and approval, or feeling good about yourself even without the benefit of recognition and praise. How does this information help to rebuild your self-esteem?

4. Think about what kinds of realistic goals to set for yourself, rather than trying to live up to impossible standards. In what ways are you learning to be more inner-directed in your assessments and values?

5. Where do you typically fall on the reaction spectrum: defensive avoidance of pain—resentment and bitterness—

angry explosion at others? Describe specific incidents as examples. How can you change any responses you dislike?

6. In what ways have you avoided joy or success, or otherwise lived down to your abuser's predictions? Are you willing to risk making changes and learn to realize your capabilities?

7. Who do you know who loves you unconditionally? Describe how you have experienced God's love for you. Have you seen him accurately? Or do you see God like you did an abusive parent?

THIRTEEN

The Making of an Abuser

✦ ✦ ✦

A LONG THE WAY WE HAVE SEEN peepholes of insight about
how verbal abuse becomes a habit. Perhaps you have
glimpsed through one of these into precisely your own scenario. In case you haven't, however, let's review in a more
detailed and organized fashion just what is required to make
a person an abuser.

YOU WERE ABUSED

The most common cause of verbal abuse is that of suffering abuse yourself. However, not everyone who suffered verbal abuse becomes an abuser. Some people are too innately
sensitive and kind. Knowing from personal experience how
painful verbal abuse can be, they go to the opposite extreme.
These people are often super-sensitive, always speak carefully, and will take abuse from others rather than even speak
up assertively.

Margaret is just such a mother. Even today, the painful
memories can bring tears to her eyes. Her parents berated
her on a regular basis. For the sake of discipline, they isolated
her and withheld all evidences of any love they may have felt
for her. She emerged from childhood afraid of people,

lonely, almost totally unable to trust anyone to love her.

Despite the immensity of her emotional damage, Margaret met a kind, considerate man. After a lengthy courtship, she finally trusted his love enough to marry him. They eventually had two lovely children. As she took growing delight in the exciting stages of their development, Margaret often wondered how her parents could have become so cruelly abusive of her. According to family photos, she, too, had once been a beautiful, lovable baby.

And then, one by one, her children reached the rebellious stage of the normal two year old. To her horror, Margaret heard someone yelling at her children. The voice sounded exactly like her mother's. It was a day of torment for this loving woman when she recognized that harsh screaming voice was her own! When she came to see me, her face as well as her voice pleaded, "Help me stop abusing my children!" It was so good to be able to assure her she could stop. In Chapter 17 you'll learn what I told her.

Even though there are exceptions, most adults who practice verbal abuse suffered similar treatment as children. They may even believe it had been good for them. Vernon was the father of an abused child with whom I worked. As I listened to his concerns about his daughter, I could tell that he cared deeply about her. I also knew his concerns were well founded. Melissa was, indeed, showing signs of serious difficulty. She was rude to her classmates and to her somewhat passive teacher. She certainly knew a great many abusive labels and her language was habitually rough.

After listening at length to Vernon's concerns, I asked how he had tried to correct Melissa's many problems. As I listened, I learned the reasons for her conduct and where she had learned the language of abuse which she spoke so frequently. Vernon described the insulting labels he used in corrrecting her and even demonstrated the harsh voice and angry face Melissa knew all too well.

In the brief time we had together, I wanted to help him see the damaging patterns of verbal abuse. So I asked the inevitable psychiatrist's question, "And Vernon, how did your parents correct you when you were a boy?" Vernon wasted no time in telling me—after informing me that all psychiatrists were nuts and only wanted to blame mothers. He went on to reveal the hard, cruel words his mother had used on him. He described even the physical abuse she had heaped upon him.

And then Vernon uttered those key, but fatal words: "Mom was rough on me, but she made a man out of me. And I figure I can make her ways work on Melissa, too!" Vainly I tried to help him discover that in the eleven years he had been practicing these methods, they had not helped his daughter. Her rudeness and aggression were worse this year than last. Her school work and personal adjustment were both suffering.

Vernon knew these facts were true and admitted that her behavior at home was also terrible. But he was certain that he only needed to try harder. He would teach Melissa. After all, Mom had certainly gotten through to him.

It is not necessary, of course, for you to live on either extreme even if you were abused. You can learn better ways.

Was I really abused? Perhaps you wonder if you really were emotionally abused. It is easy to talk yourself out of the truth and stay caught in the familiar but deadly old web of taking all the blame. Don't yield to that temptation. Remember that verbal abuse creates scars that remain throughout life. Here is a self-test that can help you to look for some typical scars.

1. Did my brothers or sisters treat me in ways that resulted in my feeling inferior, unwanted, and unloved?
2. Did I learn to feel guilty and to punish myself? Examples include hurting myself, thinking of or trying to take my life, or feeling deeply depressed.
3. Did I learn to keep quiet and withdraw from my siblings' activities?
4. Did I have nervous habits, like pulling my hair or picking at my skin, or other kinds of rituals?

5. Did I experience nightmares, frequent headaches, or stomach aches, over an extended period of time?
6. Did I, on the other hand, learn to be angry and aggressive toward my siblings or take out such feelings on others?
7. Did I have difficulty concentrating in school or even when reading a book?
8. Do I, even now, question whether such abuse was real or imagined?
9. Do I feel comfortable with my siblings now? Or do I avoid them out of fear of further attacks?
10. Do I over-identify with my own children or other children who may be verbally abused by peers?

If you answer yes to the majority of these questions, it is likely that you really were abused. Healing can only come by working through the hidden but emerging memories of these devastating experiences.

YOU FEEL POWERLESS TO STOP THE ABUSE

You may recall that children who are verbally abused literally are powerless. Whatever attempts they make to retaliate usually prompt more abuse, which may even turn into intolerable physical abuse. Such treatment creates fear that becomes so habitual that it is woven into the fiber of a child's personality. As an adult, he or she continues to feel powerless and fearful.

Yet, as an adult, one must cope with family, co-workers, neighbors, and all sorts of people in everyday life. How do *you* feel when you confront disagreements or when someone challenges your authority? Whether or not you like to admit it, you are almost certain to feel powerless if you were abused as a child. Yet in most adult situations, you dare not *act* powerless. If anything is looked down upon in today's Western culture, it is weakness. So, of course, you dare not reveal such a trait.

If you grew up being verbally abused, you are almost certain to experience a profound sense of anxiety under such circumstances. You will tend to develop an inner conflict between your fears and the demands of our culture. In today's world, people are expected to be strong, fearless, and aggressive. If you fail to fit that description, you are likely to be ridiculed and put down all over again.

Just as when you were a child, it will seem to you that you have no choice. You will be tempted to submit to the abuse, try helplessly to please your abusers, and live in silent misery. Those of you who learned to combat abuse with counterattacks will continue that habit. You will live in repeated conflicts that flare up in anger. You will feel stronger than those who attempt to be placaters. But you will find yourself feeling lonely as you end up antagonizing others. You will become as abusive as your one-time tormenters were.

The Bible gives us insight into a way out of this dilemma. Isaiah wrote, "In returning and rest you shall be saved. In quietness and confidence shall be your strength" (Is 30:15, NKJV). Find the time to become quiet and reconsider your past. Think about the nearness of a God who is infinite in strength and wisdom, who loves you unconditionally. You can safely rest in that ever-present source of help.

One of the tragedies of abuse lies in the fact that the parents' betrayal of a child's trust makes it difficult to trust the heavenly Father. Overcoming that misperception, however, is possible. One of my best ways to get in touch with God is to study nature. If you explore astronomy, geology, biology, and botany, you see such order and beauty that you begin to perceive the greatness of God in a new way. You can tap into that inexhaustible strength when your own seems lacking.

You also need to remember that there is more of that strength within you than you may realize. You only need to recognize and develop it. Just as exercise strengthens your physical muscles, so using your faith—instead of giving in to your weaknesses—will develop your spiritual resources.

STRESS PILES UP

While writing this book, I am facing six major sources of stress encompassing just about every facet of my life. The build-up of stress results in unique symptoms as varied as individuals, yet similar in basic categories. These include physical signs such as sleeplessness, eating problems, muscular stiffness and pain, headaches, and stomach aches, to name only a few.

Stress also manifests itself through emotional distress—worry and anxiety, irritability and moodiness, and sometimes the cover-up, which is anger. When anger becomes intense enough, it is likely to be expressed through verbal abuse. Sadly enough, verbal abuse is most commonly dumped upon the family. The ones we love most seem to offer a safe outlet, so our anger may be displaced on them when it really belongs at work or elsewhere.

All of us, however, know people in the workplace who regularly let out their frustration on the job. Perhaps you are the victim of such abuse. A young friend of mine told me only recently that her office is afflicted with one such person. Gretchen herself is a gentle woman who tends to absorb the shock waves of such abuse. Her very vulnerability made her all the more likely a target of this supervisor's venomous words.

The verbal abuse was worse some times than at others, but over an extended period, Gretchen accumulated enough information to help her understand this person. She learned that her supervisor suffered from a form of mental illness. During his stressful times, he decompensated—much like a damaged heart does when it must work too hard. It was at these times that the abuse was heaped upon the employees.

When my friend understood the basic problem, it helped her cope much more successfully. Gretchen no longer took the abuse personally and tried to help her co-workers be less susceptible to his anger and more supportive. They began to speak up to him in clear but positive ways which he respected. Gradually the atmosphere of the entire office improved.

Even when you are the target of unfair verbal abuse, there are some things you can do to cope. Not only will you be better off, but you may help those around you—including the abuser. When stress builds up for you, what is your solution? Certainly you do not want to take out the frustrations of your stress on people you love. But what *can* you do? Here are some possible answers.

1. Recognize and clearly identify your stress. My recent stress build-up, for example, included an impending book manuscript deadline, a dear relative who was diagnosed with cancer, the arrival of licensing and accreditation entities where I work, the chronic inadequacy of time, and several other, smaller stresses. Many times, we live with stress so routinely that we fail to realize that it is accumulating.
2. Make a plan for dealing with each component of your stress. Include budgeting of time, disciplining yourself to say no to some things, and asking for help.
3. Take charge of your life. You need some exercise to cope with the build-up of over twenty stress hormones, chemicals which your body manufactures in its endocrine system to provide the energy you need to deal with stress. Exercise will help metabolize these chemicals so you will not have as many physical symptoms. Eat properly with a balance in protein, carbohydrates, and fats. Avoid fad diets and excessive weight loss or gain. Schedule your time to get enough sleep, and by all means, work out time for some play and laughter!
4. Find a friend and confidante. When you share your stress with someone who cares about you, the burden becomes so much lighter. Be considerate, of course! Don't overburden your friend with your concerns. And be wise! Don't seek a friend who is currently carrying more burdens to

unload on you than you already have. Exchanging your concerns with one another is a major benefit of friendship.

5. Don't be afraid to seek professional counsel. Many of your concerns can be dealt with on your own, so I do not recommend running for help for every small anxiety. But on the other extreme, neither do you need to be reluctant to get counsel when your life seems out of control.

6. Learn to look ahead. The day to day struggle may seem unbearable, but gaining perspective and a long-range view of life will offer hope. The illness will pass, the time pressures can be eased, the deadlines will pass—and you will survive. You will even discover care-freeness and peace once again.

By learning to deal with your stress, you will be much less likely to become abusive. And you will be gaining the priceless qualities of wisdom and strength that will help you overcome the heartaches of your own abuse.

YOU LOSE SELF-CONTROL

This loss of self-control especially needs to be addressed in today's Western culture. For nearly two decades we have lived with the motto, "Let it all hang out." Self-expression is encouraged, even if it is not well understood. Parents are warned not to inhibit the expression of feelings by their children, lest it stunt their emotional and psychological growth.

Now some of that philosophy makes sense to me. I was raised in an era when it seemed permissible for my parents to express their feelings intensely. But somehow, it was not okay for *me* to do that. I know I became a moody and angrily withdrawn child for some years because I had no avenue for expressing my needs or feelings. I clearly and subjectively see the need for such opportunities.

The pendulum, however, has swung too far to the opposite extreme. The young adults who have grown up through these years of free expression are commonly verbally abusive. To their teachers, employers, and peers, they respond similarly—in verbal attacks that are often devastating. Even when suspended from school or dismissed from a job, they seem imperturbable. As long as they can speak their own minds, they seem indifferent to the pain they inflict on others, or may even take perverse pleasure in that pain.

You may be one of those people who are abused by someone like this. Be very certain that you understand that a basic element of such abusers is poor self-control. Such persons can vent their anger so intensely that you may become intimidated by them and even believe you are somehow at fault.

That is rarely the case in this category of abusers. They are simply overgrown bullies who were never taught the marvelous value of self-control. Your response to them is crucial. If you act afraid of them, that fear feeds their pathological, negative power, and their abusive behavior will become worse. Counterattacking, on the other hand, rarely results in victory.

A psychiatrist friend of mine likens all people to two food items. One is the category of *apples*. Apples have a skin to protect them, a layer of delicious pulp that is nourishing and sweet, and most important, an inner core. In that vital center are the living seeds that can create new apple trees and more apples.

The other food with which he compares people is the *onion*. Onions have very little skin. They have layer upon layer of crisp tissue. When any onion is hurt by cutting, it sends out a chemical that stings the eyes and causes tears to flow. And there are no seeds in the core of an onion.

People who lack self-control are like the onion. It takes only a little cut to set the toxic substance loose. But that toxin is so powerful it can stimulate many tears. Once you understand and recognize these "onion" people, you can protect yourself.

First of all, remember they are not out to get you! They are simply so unprotected that they have learned to hold others at arm's length so they themselves won't be hurt. Most people learn to treat "onions" very carefully or just stay away from them. You may do this yourself in order to keep from being abused.

Your best response to this type of abuser is the clear, gently strong statement of the real facts. Then ignore the person and the abusive words. When he or she is reasonably courteous, respond positively. You may not change such "onion" people, but you need not not give them the power to hurt you either.

YOU BECOME DEPRESSED AND EXPLODE IN ANGER

One of the major emotional ingredients of depression is anger. Even the process of grief includes the stage of anger. When grieving or depressed people give vent to that anger, it may very well be expressed as verbal abuse.

Chuck is a clear example of such abuse. He had suffered a series of immense losses. In his need to be strong and manly, he had refused any comfort or help. Chuck could handle everything, and in no uncertain terms, he made that fact known. One evening, this tower of strength was especially grouchy. His wife tried to talk with him but he replied in grunts and monosyllables. Hilary began to suspect she had offended him in some way. Her questions regarding that possibility were also answered with a shake of Chuck's head or another grunt.

Tired of her queries and probing, Chuck yelled, "Hilary, can't you see I don't want to talk? Or are you too stupid and selfish to recognize the truth? I can take care of myself! Just leave me alone! I don't need you to mother me!"

All too often cast in the role of mothering against her wishes, Hilary felt she had blown it again. Wanting to help, she had gone too far. She must be a terrible wife when she wanted to be the best! Hilary left the room and tried to lose herself in a book. But the tension between her spouse and herself was too great. There had to be some release.

After much thought, she trudged back to the chair in which Chuck was still sitting—moody and angry, yet strangely sad, too. She showed genuine compassion for him but was also honest about her pain at Chuck's painful words. "Chuck," Hilary stated, "there's something very wrong between us and I don't like it. I know you're troubled about something, and I don't want to pry. Let me assure you, neither do I want to mother you! But I do want to be your friend. Let me know how I can help."

With these calm and forgiving words, Chuck's defenses crumbled. He poured out the woes of his day and the many days before that. And he allowed Hilary to hold him briefly. Then he stated an opinion shared by many men. "Thanks, Hilary. But I'm a man. I should be strong enough to handle these problems." And again he withdrew into the armor of his "macho" image. Not only were Chuck's words abusive, but his attitude inflicted pain on Hilary as well. His wife had so much to offer him in understanding and comfort. But he rejected her offer and shut her out of an area of great need.

Chuck's abusive words had exploded out of his bout with depression. But he did not suddenly happen to express his depression abusively. Having grown up with a father who made much of being strong, Chuck had translated his vulnerable feelings into angry, aggressive words and actions. He, too, must be strong.

Indeed, verbal abuse must be taught. Whether it is through one avenue or another, the abuser has learned this destructive habit from someone else. He or she then repeats the mistakes, unwittingly teaching them to the next generation, and spreading them like a contagious disease to those nearby.

Now let's take a look at you—perhaps yourself the long-term victim of verbal abuse. Is it possible that without your conscious awareness, you could be an abuser? Surely not! But let's examine that question more closely.

✦ ✦ ✦

Study Questions

1. As the victim of verbal abuse, have you responded more by becoming abusive yourself or by being super-sensitive and careful in asserting yourself? Describe some incidents which typify your behavior.

2. What efforts have you made to change habits of verbal abuse? Have you experienced success or powerlessness?

3. How do circumstances that flare up in anger make you feel? Do you experience a profound sense of anxiety and inner conflict?

4. What kinds of physical symptoms or emotional distress do you experience as the result of stress? How do you handle such stress?

5. How do you express anger? Describe any incidents in which you recognize the pattern of becoming grouchy and depressed, and then exploding in angry, abusive words and/or actions.

6. After angry explosions, many people experience great guilt. Do you? Have you learned to unload guilt through forgiveness and restitution?

FOURTEEN

Are You an Abuser?

✦ ✦ ✦

WHEN I WAS A CHILD, I repeatedly vowed that I would never scream at my children. And I rarely did. But I can, with horrifying clarity, recall a number of times when I behaved in exactly the way I so firmly determined I would never do. On those unfortunate occasions, I did indeed yell ugly words at my children.

I would give almost anything if I could reverse those home movies in my memory and take back those harsh words. The tragedy of verbal abuse lies in that very fact—it can never be erased. Forgiveness and healing can be achieved, thankfully, but the scars are there for life!

With such an absolutely firm commitment, if I could abuse those dear to me, so could you. In this chapter, we'll take a look at such a possibility and how you can determine if you are an abuser. Are you a strict, no-nonsense parent? Are you a hard worker, trying to put out an honest day's work and endeavoring to motivate your co-workers? Are you just trying to be assertive and outspoken? Or are you a verbal abuser? Let's consider some revealing questions.

DO PEOPLE TEND TO AVOID YOU?

If people tend to avoid you, such a discovery might be true for many reasons. They may prefer their own privacy. You may be so competent that they are jealous and resentful of your excellence. Maybe you talk too much or are too quiet and people are a bit uncomfortable with you. Perhaps you remind another person of some difficult individual he or she has known.

But if none of these ideas seem to fit you, perhaps you should take a look at how you treat others. Perhaps you see yourself as being simply honest to the point of being blunt. You may take pride in what you see as opinions and directness. Indeed, there is much to be said for these qualities.

If, however, you find acquaintances unwilling to become friends or your friends finding reasons to limit their time with you, something more may be going on. If you recall on their faces evidence of distress during conversations, it could be that you are verbally abusive. The line between frankness and abuse is a fine one and you may not realize when you have crossed it.

Marie was such an abusive person. In nearly every conversation, at least one person was left in emotional shambles by her caustic words. To a mother who had to work to care for her children, she said, "I feel so sorry for children who have no mother. In our world people are so materialistic!" Her words to another woman who was suffering abandonment by a wayward husband were, "Well! I know there's always another side to such a story. If wives only treated their husbands right, they wouldn't have to look elsewhere!" You can understand why Marie had very few friends.

If you see a bit of yourself in Marie, ask your friends how they perceive you. Do they hear your comments as an attack of sorts? Are your friends left feeling confused at best after spending time with you? If so, by all means change your ways. Get help if you need it, but do not go on hurting people with your words.

ARE CHILDREN AFRAID OF YOU?

In today's often cruel world, well-meaning parents are anxious to teach respect to their children. No one can argue against the great need to do exactly that. But with growing frequency I see parents who mistake respect for fear. They go well beyond the boundary of knowing and setting limits and consequences. Their children are clearly afraid of the verbal abuse of their parents.

Let me remind you once more of the elements of verbal abuse: insulting the personhood of another person (for example, "You're worthless"), creating a situation in which the other feels helpless, and leaving emotional scars that influence a person's entire life. Such a process is usually based on intense anger that in itself is overwhelming. Over time, especially with little children, that anger creates either great intimidation or a growing rebellion.

Intimidation means that your child withdraws from you and may become afraid of all adults. He or she feels not only powerless, but also worthless and cannot develop the core of self-esteem that is so essential to any sort of success.

More worrisome, but actually healthier, is the rebellion many children develop. They refuse to cower in fear, so they talk back, usually rudely, or stubbornly rebel through silence. Many parents cannot tolerate such rudeness and punish these strong-willed children even to the point of physical abuse. They never see the mirroring of their own harsh attitudes and fail to recognize their role in teaching this reaction to their children.

Perhaps you and your children have established a sort of equilibrium—as uneasy as that may be. But you may recognize that your children make each other cry by teasing or name calling, for example. Furthermore, they lack on-going friendships in school or in the neighborhood. You occasionally have calls from your school staff complaining about your child's abusiveness. *You* may see your child as an assertive leader who is afraid of no one. But look again. It is just possible that you have missed an important signal that by your own example, your child has become abusive.

Recently, I overheard an older parent with her adult daughter. The woman had done an excellent performance in an amateur musical show. After telling her daughter she had done well, the mother began to list the ways she could have done better. As the mother spoke, I could see the crestfallen look on her daughter's face intensify. Once again, I suspect, she felt she had failed. She would never be good enough.

Actually, her mother knew infinitely less about her instrument than the performer did. She simply could not refrain from criticizing her adult child. Was this painful to the musician? Did it create a climate in which she felt inept and worthless? Did it create and deepen emotional scars? Certainly it did. With good intentions of making her daughter perfect, this mother was verbally abusing her.

DOES YOUR SPOUSE AVOID YOU?

Stuart, a highly skilled office manager, found himself dreading evenings. He loved his home. His wife had made it both comfortable and attractive. While he was well-organized and respected at work, Stu had always hurried home because he loved to just be there. Julie worked also, and when he could, he would surprise her by beginning dinner or vacuuming the house. They hoped to have children someday, but now there was just the two of them. They could do all the romantic, spontaneous things they chose. Life was carefree and easy.

But slowly, insidiously, things were changing. Julie became more critical of the mess Stuart made in her immaculate kitchen than she was appreciative of his meals. She was critical of the rounded "tummy" his contentment was allowing him to develop. She noticed his hair was a tiny bit thin on top and told him about it. And whatever he did to try to help around the house was never good enough.

When Julie criticized Stuart, she found new derogatory

terms for him. "Slob," "stupid," "fat," and "selfish" were only some of the nicer terms. She had no interest in his affections and told him clearly that she was through with sex unless he shaped up. Her demeanor was one of disgust, far worse for Stu to handle than if she had shown outright anger.

Without realizing it, this hen-pecked husband began to stay late at work. He always had telephone calls to make and it suddenly seemed easier to make them from the office than at home as he used to do. While his desk was cluttered, Stu was more relaxed and peaceful there than at home. He had come to dread the next painful onslaught of condemnation from Julie.

Other late workers began to suggest evening activities to Stuart. He joined a bowling league and a softball team. Before he was fully aware of what was happening, Stu was gone most of the evenings. Julie further berated her husband for his lack of attention to her and continued to criticize him in every way.

Julie herself had an extremely demanding job. It required perfection and she pushed herself to achieve the success for which she had trained for so long. Julie did not intend to demand that same absolute perfection from her husband, but there it was. She was exacting from him the same super-excellence that she did from herself. And in the unrelenting drive for that topmost rung in the success ladder, Julie had unwittingly become a shrew—a verbally abusive wife.

Even though Julie had suffered abuse from her parents and her boss, she was now passing it along to her husband. She did not like this trait in others, but to her horror she faced the fact that she had become what she hated.

Here are a few questions that can help you discover if you, too, have been an abusive spouse.

1. Are you feeling a growing sense of irritation with your spouse?
2. Along with this negative attitude, are you aware that he or she really isn't so bad?

3. Do you feel, in fact, somewhat remorseful or guilty about the things you say to your spouse?
4. Above all, are you sensing that your spouse is drifting away from you?

Now don't jump too quickly to the certainty that any such drift is directly stemming from your abuse! There are many reasons for spouses to grow apart. But right now check out your attitudes and actions with the above questions. If you must answer affirmatively, you need to make changes. We'll discuss how to do that later.

DO YOU LEAVE CONFRONTATIONS FEELING ASHAMED OR GUILTY?

Guilt and shame are commonly shared emotions which follow in the wake of a variety of situations. Many of us, in fact, lay unnecessary guilt trips on ourselves. We blame ourselves no matter what we do and keep that sense of shame activated much of the time. This is false guilt, easily unloaded by accurate information and a fair attitude.

But real guilt is actually one of your best allies. It will notify you that you really are doing something wrong—something that is hurting people around you and that will bring serious damage to your own character.

Much of my life I had learned to be super-submissive, giving in to everyone around me even when that was not in the best interest of anyone. When I finally broke out of that mold, the change required great effort. I was excited to discover, however, that I had a good mind and worthwhile ideas.

For some months, I reveled in speaking my mind—in anger or tears, I didn't care which. But then I began to feel vaguely uneasy. Just as I've written above, some of my friends began to stray away. My children seemed uncertain as to who their mom had become. Worst of all, I began to feel that sharp edge of guilt and shame. After a board meeting, for example, I would drive home feeling uneasy—as if I had been too pushy, too determined to have a decision go my way. Having been carried away in proving my new-found power, I had lost sight of what was really best.

The truth became abundantly clear at last, and I didn't like the new me after all! Fortunately, I caught the trend before I had lost all my friends and my own self-respect. But I was just as vulnerable to becoming verbally abusive as anyone else—a very healthy sort of humility for anyone to gain. Only when I realized that I was on the verge of verbally abusing those I cherished could I quit my damaging behavior.

This point needs a little more in-depth explanation. My own personal history made it extremely clear to me that giving in to everyone is not a healthy practice. I heard and believed, on the other hand, that we need to confront people. We are taught to be open and honest. These are certainly valid and useful qualities. According to my own experience and conscious intentions, I was trying desperately to be assertive and to practice healthy confrontation. What actually happened was neither! In the intensity of my efforts, I hated to admit that I had crossed the line into verbal abuse.

Once again, the definition of verbal abuse can help to clarify one's situation. Words and attitudes are abusive when they belittle another, leave him/her feeling helpless, inflict pain that is not forgotten, and in some degree permanently affect the other person in a negative manner. Remember to always check out your attitudes as well as your words. Be certain they are aimed at the best for everyone, not at the transient power of having your own way!

Healthy confrontation includes these elements:

1. A clear conception of issues, including a broad overview.
2. An open mind that is willing to accept and check out new information.
3. An inner certainty of your good-will for people involved in the issues—whether or not you particularly *like* them.
4. A willingness to speak your mind clearly and emphati-

cally, as well as the willingness to listen equally atten-
tively to others' emphatic statements.

5. The ability to accept decisions graciously—even when
you are not totally in agreement—and work out the
agreed upon solutions.

Ask yourself these questions. Am I proud of being blunt,
even cruelly honest? Does this practice lose friends I once
held dear? Above all, do I feel that subtle sense of disquiet
after a disagreement? When I confront someone, do I later
realize that I out-powered him or her? And did I do that
maneuvering in a way that made the other person feel
stupid, worthless, or helpless? How wonderful it is to discover that you've been hurting people—because now you
can change!

ARE YOUR NEGATIVE FEELINGS INTENSE?

To understand this issue, let me call on my years of experience with children. When I worked as a pediatrician, I examined many hundreds of newborn babies. I discovered a
fact that has opened up for me vast areas of knowledge and
understanding.

Babies are born with only two emotions, both of which are
extremely powerful. One is anger and the other is fear. Whenever a baby experiences pain, it will express the cry of anger—
unmistakable, intense indignation. The very process of birth
is itself excruciatingly painful. And every healthy newborn
gives that reassuring yell of anger at the insult of it all.

As babies grow and mature throughout childhood and
ultimately into adulthood, the pain expands from physical
to emotional in all the range of events and interactions that
cause hurt. That cry of rage may become silent when we
grow up, but a feeling of anger is always some sort of protection for the hurt and helplessness of pain of any kind. Anger
feels so powerful.

Fear is also present at birth, identifiable by its unique

body response and the piercing cry of the panic that only uninhibited babies demonstrate. As babies mature, they become accustomed to all sorts of loud noises and sudden movements which had originally prompted that cry of fear. But there is in everyone the residual fear that can become healthy caution, crippling panic, or even a sanity-threatening phobia.

I learned as a pediatrician and a psychiatrist that people do not tolerate fear as well as they do anger. Fear by its very definition seems weak and even powerless. The fear generated by emotional abuse is most likely to be hidden under an overlay of anger. That outcome is logical because of anger's deceptive sense of power, an acceptable antidote for fear.

This cover-up of fear by anger (or aggression) is exactly the mechanism that accounts for the constant renewal of the habits of abuse. Rather than shrink in fear, people learn to counterattack in anger.

How sad that few people stop to consider how love is imparted to babies! It is in love and through the love of others that one learns to love. When infants receive too little love, they fail to learn how to give it. That means they are left with primarily aggression and fear. If fear becomes paramount, the child is likely to react against abuse by withdrawing and heroically attempting to placate others. If, however, he or she develops patterns of aggression, the likelihood of being abusive is great.

If you want to know whether you are an abusive person, you may discover the truth by analyzing yourself a bit. Are you typically fearful? A placator who works for peace at all costs? Or are you one who has learned to overcome your fears by being even more angry than those who verbally abused you? Neither extreme is healthy!

How wonderful it will be when you discover that fear can best be overcome through love. It's never too late to learn that great love alleviates the pain and heals the emotional scars of abuse!

Study Questions

1. Do you become intensely angry at people when you disagree with them or are offended by them?

2. When you are angry, do you verbally and emotionally explode, lashing out at your target?

3. In such explosions, do you speak primarily in "you" messages? For example, "You are so stupid! You'll never do anything right!" "You make me sick!"

4. For a little while after such an explosion, do you feel powerful and even relieved?

5. Later on, are you aware of remorse and feelings of guilt? Do you dread seeing the target of your anger the next time?

6. Do you at times direct similar anger at your own self, feeling a sense of relief from what you see as deserved punishment?

7. Do your family and friends appear afraid when you feel angry? Do they scurry away from you at the times you are upset?

8. Do you, in fact, find yourself losing friends?

If you find to your horror that you can answer many of these questions positively, take heart! You can do something about stopping abuse, both in others and yourself. We will tackle this topic in the last section of this book.

Part Four

Combatting
Verbal Abuse

FIFTEEN

Coping with the Pain

✦ ✦ ✦

W E HAVE ALREADY SEEN HOW EASY IT IS to become an abuser by trying to combat an abusive person. Such direct efforts obviously do not provide a simple answer to the question, "How do I deal with verbal abuse?" But there are answers.

If you are the victim of verbal abuse, let's first think about how you can cope with the pain and helplessness you suffer at the mouth of another person. Some brief suggestions have already been made throughout the book about relating to your abuser. Now is the time to go into more detail about coping within yourself and then with the abusive person you must handle. You can find the healing that will restore or create sanity in your world.

BUILD YOUR OWN SELF-RESPECT

The lack of an adequate sense of self-worth is one of the most basic ingredients in being vulnerable to verbal abuse. When you *believe* the hurtful statements of another against you, it is because you unconsciously already suspect those negative qualities are actually part of you.

Almost invariably, those beliefs so critical of yourself go back to the beginnings of your life. The most common factors that create and nurture a low sense of worth are these.

1. You believe you were a burden or problem to your parents. The parents who told their child that she was an "accident" are a good example. Since she was born late in her mother's child-bearing years, they may have simply meant to explain why she was so much younger than her next older sister. But what she heard was, "You were not planned, not wanted, not accepted, not needed."

2. Any child who hears parents bickering about who should take care of him or her feels unwanted. With so many homes where both parents are employed outside the home, many children often hear their parents arguing about who should miss work when a child is ill. When this kind of situation arises, the resulting feeling of being a burden can only add to children's devaluation of themselves. What does it say to children that neither parent wants to be with them, even when they are ill?

A well-known child psychologist says that parents need to do more than just love their children. They need to be "in love" with them. That quality of being "in love" means a person craves to be near the object of that love. The loved one is seen as desirable, clever, gifted, and beautiful. Now few people are always so glamorous, but that is how children need to be treated.

3. If you missed out on this good stuff, you are likely to feel that was because of your own badness. Amy suffered ongoing emotional neglect as a child. Even now in middle age, she feels unimportant and unwanted. The abusive labels with which she grew up have left their scars. She recalls terms like "ugly," "clumsy," "wallflower," and "sickly." To this very day, her ears are closed to more loving descriptors like "precious," "helpful," or "brilliant"—even though she is all of these and much more.

But Amy is unwilling to live out her life with these negative beliefs about herself. She is learning to believe she is loved and loving, capable and achieving, and even beautiful. She has had to review and revise her entire philosophy of life, a process that takes time and requires help in many cases.

LEARN TO UNDERSTAND YOURSELF

It may seem difficult to really *love and accept* yourself at first. So start with *understanding* yourself. Begin keeping a daily journal or recording your thoughts and feelings on tape. Reread or listen to your own insights about yourself now and about your past and the events that shaped your life.

As you gain a perspective on all of these elements, you will begin to perceive the many good qualities you possess. You will never be bad enough to merit those harsh words that left such scars in your heart. You will understand that those abusive people were hurt themselves, and were passing on the results of someone else's mistakes.

Everyone needs correction at times, but never abuse. Furthermore, the misbehaviors of your past have meaning. These childish attempts to express a need or a feeling require help and guidance more than punishment. This point is a delicate one, because you may easily be tempted to place blame on others and excuse yourself too much. In order to grow in positive ways, you must accept the fact that everyone makes mistakes. These errors need to be corrected and the necessary steps of forgiveness must be learned.

As you begin to understand your needs and your emotions, you can find more healthy ways to meet those needs and express those emotions. There are four simple steps in doing this:

1. Put into words how you feel and what you need.
2. Determine what it will require to meet the need.
3. Make an action plan that effectively takes care of the need.
4. Follow through with that plan!

As you learn more about your strengths, you will feel less like a helpless victim. And as you make this significant change in yourself, others will miraculously see you differently as well. They will begin to respect you more as you learn to feel better about yourself.

There is one notable exception to this philosophy. Paula was an example of a person who suffered severely from verbal abuse all of her life. She felt extremely badly about herself and was dependent on others to help her feel at least good enough to drag through her days. She became expecially attached to one dear friend.

When Paula began to discover her strengths, she became slowly and surely more healthy and independent. The friend could not understand the changes Paula was making. She felt threatened and abandoned. Paula had to make a choice, at last—stop her exciting growth, or lose the friend who could relate with her only as a total dependent.

LEARN TO BE ASSERTIVE

Once you begin to respect yourself and recognize your good qualities, you can risk becoming assertive. Whole books and extensive college courses have been created to teach assertiveness. But let's think about it simply.

Webster's Dictionary defines "assert" this way: "to state positively, declare, affirm; to maintain or defend (rights or claims, etc.)." A further definition of asserting oneself is listed as: "1. to insist on one's rights or on being recognized; and 2. to thrust oneself forward."

The Latin root word for assert is "ad," meaning "to," plus "serere," meaning to join or bind. And that is just what healthy assertiveness does. It binds you to others by making them aware of you. It enables them to see you as a person with ideas, feelings, and needs that are worthy of respect—not abuse.

As I have observed the great push toward assertiveness

training, I must confess one area of concern—the ease with which one who has been abused can cross over the line of assertiveness into aggression. As I have thought in depth about the risks involved in going beyond assertiveness, I have clarified an idea that I hope you will find useful.

Aggression is highly likely to involve abuse of others, perhaps as a form of retaliation or getting even. It is no good if people trade their own abuse for the abuse of someone else. As I've explained before, such trade-offs are common among abused people. By contrast, *assertiveness*, according to its best definition, is "to state *positively*, declare, or affirm." It results in maintaining or defending one's rights or claims. When you express yourself in such a constructive manner, others can hardly fail to respect you, and you surely will respect yourself.

When you sit in slavish silence and allow others to insult and abuse you, you may be hurting them as well as yourself. When we allow others to speak abusively without challenging them, we are giving tacit consent to their cruelty. They are likely to abuse others as well as you. So it is certainly not being selfish or rude to speak up to such people. It is the manner in which you speak up that is crucial. Assertive language states *positively* what you think, observe, and feel. It states clearly what *you* need and does so without offending others.

Good assertiveness is also tenacious. When I was learning to apply this important concept in my own life, there were times when I would make one attempt to express my own needs and feelings—usually a pretty feeble one at that—and then revert to my old habit of silent withdrawal. My reticence demanded a very receptive and sensitive person to even hear my weak effort at speaking up.

As I learned to be more insistent, you may recall, I endured a period of time when I suspect I was downright obnoxious! I spoke up with great intensity and held out to the often bitter end. Some of those memories create a sense of embarrassment in me now, but I'm very glad I took the risk of making such mistakes. Through my subjective experiences of both extremes of withdrawal and aggressiveness, I have been able to reach my own comfort zone of clear, positive assertiveness.

Don't be afraid to explore ways in which you, too, can change. Doing such work consciously and carefully will enable you to find your own zone of comfort!

LET OTHERS BE YOUR MIRROR

When you groom yourself, you need a mirror to reflect the smudges and flaws in your appearance if you are to look respectable. We have exactly the same need when we clean up our old ways of taking abuse or being abusive. Old habits are powerful and it is that very strength that perpetuates them.

As you observe others, let them become a mirror to you. You will see abusive people almost every day. And you will equally see their victims—those who unwittingly feed into this cycle of hurt and withdrawal *or* retaliation. You can clearly define in others what initiates the abuse, how it is carried out, and how painful are the results.

Once you understand this process, think about ways in which this vicious cycle could be changed in those you have observed. Then place your own self in the light of their mirror and apply what you've learned from your observations to yourself. How can you react differently? What do you need to stop the process of abuse that has made your life miserable?

BE COURAGEOUS

People learn to submit to verbal abuse out of fear. They learn to be silent because such a response usually curtails the flow of those painful words. Overcoming abuse, even as an adult, demands great courage. It is not just the here and now event that we must battle, but the collection of countless similar events that painfully echo from our past.

How can we be the match for those powerful others who taught us to take their abuse? It is indeed a frightening prospect! Speak up? Declare? Affirm positively? These are at first a foreign language, but one which can be learned. You will be surprised how quickly you can master it and how positive the results will be.

The first step is always the most difficult, but as in my own experience, this process demands enough tenacity to explore both extremes—both the fearful withdrawal and the aggressive attack. With time and the courage to face the struggle, you will be well on your way out of the abuse you have endured.

BE PROFOUNDLY HONEST

One of the most common psychological practices is that of seeing in others something of ourselves. We call this mechanism "projection." Sometimes such thinking is beneficial. We see in others the honesty, optimism, and warmth that we ourselves value and cultivate. At other times, however, we may believe that others are like those who abused us. We may even project on them the fear, anger, and counter-aggression that we experience.

Thus, as I have tried to explain throughout this book, we can set up a repeat cycle of the original abuse we suffered. We expect verbal abuse and thereby *unconsciously* set it up. We do this by our attitudes and our behaviors, out of the sheer force of habit.

If you mean business about changing the abuse habits—either your own or those of others dear to you—then you must face these facts. You must be utterly honest with yourself. These questions will help you to look clearly at the role you yourself learned to play in the abuse cycle.

1. Did and do you passively take the abuse, silently giving unhealthy power to your abusers?
2. Or do you act angry and take out on others the attacks you endured in such a way as to keep the abuse going?
3. Finally, have you made excuses for others' abusiveness so that they have come to believe it's permissible to hurt you—that nothing is wrong with such practices?

In order to get others to change, you need to change first. And even if the abuser in your life doesn't change, you can! That's the exciting fact about stopping abuse! You have the right and the power to stop taking it.

You must remember two facts that can hardly be reiterated enough. First, you do not deserve abuse! No one does. You may need correction at times, but that must not be abusive. Second, it is bad for anyone to be allowed to abuse you—or anyone else. So your commitment to breaking the habits of abuse is of utmost importance.

You may not believe at first that you have the power to stop another person from being verbally abusive, but let me share with you the story of Ned and Priscilla. Priscilla made the classic choice for her marriage. She had grown up with a critical, screaming mother whom she felt she could never please. During her courtship with Ned, she vaguely felt his power to control her through his habits of criticism and fault-finding. But it seemed they could always work things out and restore harmony. Nevertheless, it was with some misgiving that she finally married Ned.

Not long after their honeymoon, Pris realized her vague fears were well-founded. On their way to a potluck supper with friends, her carefully prepared casserole spilled onto the floor of their car. Ned had been in a hurry and was driving too fast, turning sharply and braking abruptly. Pris had tried to hold the hot casserole dish steady, but inevitably some of its contents had spilled out.

Ned's temper, shortened by his hurrying to be on time, flared. For the rest of the drive he berated his wife for being so stupid, careless, and critical of his driving. (She had asked him to slow down to avoid the very event that happened!) Pris, conditioned by her many years as the focus of her mother's condemnation, accepted Ned's tirade as the truth. She apologized, promised to clean the car, and assured him she'd never take such a casserole anywhere again. At last he calmed down and was his charming self throughout the evening.

There followed years of Ned taking out on his wife his daily frustrations. If he felt less than powerful, he could shore up his sagging ego by finding some fault with Pris. And she unwittingly reinforced his negative, destructive power by at first feebly presenting her defense, then inevitably weeping, apologizing, and promising to do better.

The day finally came when Pris awoke from this nightmare of verbal abuse. She began to realize that she truly was a fine and capable woman, and there was no valid reason for her husband's tirades. She could also see that Ned was growing worse and even treating their children with verbal cruelty.

One night, Pris was cooking dinner when Ned arrived home from a short errand and stomped into the kitchen. Having stumbled on the step and twisted his ankle, he began in his old style to angrily blame her and berate her for failing to turn on the porch light. He obviously could walk, so Pris knew he was not seriously injured.

For the very first time in her life, Priscilla recognized the scenario in which she had played the victim role all of her life. Instead of her habitual apology, explanations, and helpless tears, she actually laughed. Fortunately she touched Ned in a sympathetic gesture; but nonetheless, she laughed. After a moment of consternation, Ned finally recognized the absurdity of his blaming, abusive words. He even had the grace to join Pris' laughter.

Had her abusive husband not seen the truth, Pris nevertheless would have been correct in her response. She avoided laughing *at* Ned—which constitutes abuse in its own right—

yet helped him see how ridiculously he had behaved. He could have turned on the light himself as he left on his errand so that it would have lighted his way. Had he not been in such a hurry, he could have avoided the fall. His stumble was not Pris' fault!

The secret in the change, obviously, was not in the abusive husband. The change in this case was Priscilla's growth in self-respect, insight, and courage. Her basic kindliness enabled her to express this new response in positive humor. Her transformation was the beginning of the end of verbal abuse for both of them.

FORM A NEW SET OF EXPECTATIONS

Understandably, we all tend to live up to the expectations of others who are important to us. Nancy had a math teacher in her middle school years who enjoyed an outstanding reputation among his students. Math is usually a very unpopular subject, so one day I asked my friend how it happened that her teacher was so well liked. Furthermore, most of his students earned reasonably good grades and many did very well.

After a moment's consideration, Nancy had the answer to my question. This man had a rare quality that Nancy defined this way: "He always expected us to do well. He even expected us to behave well. He showed us so much respect that we just wanted to please him."

If you want to stop being abused, you will find help through formulating a new set of expectations. When you quit expecting the worst, your facial expression and posture will look more positive. Your tone of voice will probably evidence a new degree of energy. And your behavior will demonstrate your new confidence. As you exhibit self-respect and consistently expect only the best, you will be much more likely to get it.

Such a change in you will not take place overnight. Any

worthwhile change takes time, many weeks of it. It demands a great deal of energy and you are likely to become discouraged. But don't give up!

FIVE STEPS TO CHANGE

Having made some major changes in my own outlook on life and response to hard times has yielded many profound insights. I am excited to share the steps I have learned that are required to make any significant change in a person's life.

1. Face the need to change. Even if not so emotionally healthy, it is easier to stick with old, familiar habits. Facing the facts of verbal abuse is painful, and even more so, facing your own part in this vicious cycle. You will not want to admit the truth that someone you love—or wish you could love!— is a verbal abuser. You certainly are not going to want to admit that *you* may be an abuser yourself. But you are not likely to make any significant change until you become honest enough to face the truth and courageous enough to bear the pain!

2. Give yourself permission to change. We all become as we are because of the influence of others in our lives—parents, teachers, and other authorities. Our perception of their expectations and commands helps form our habits. In few areas of life is this more true than in verbal abuse. To change abusive patterns demands that one recognize the error in such habits and then acknowledge the right to break them.

Permission to change is usually initiated by an authority figure as powerful in the present as the old authorities were in the past. Eventually, of course, one must gain such power over one's own self! You may very well find in a professional counselor such a positive authority figure. Sometimes a loyal, trustworthy friend can fulfill that function, or perhaps a clergyman or member of your family. Whatever you must do, gain the firm, clear permission to make the changes you need.

3. Develop a plan. The more I work in the counseling profession, the more I believe that change comes from two major areas: first, the insight that recognizes problems and understands them; and second, the will and self-discipline that break old habits and form new ones. To achieve the will and discipline demands a well-formulated plan.

Such a plan must include specific words you will use, preparation for the positive confrontations it will take, and resources for the courage and feedback you need to process your progress. The more specific your plan is, the more successful you will be in carrying it out. A friend is most helpful in talking through and spelling out your plan.

4. Seek trusted assistance. If you are serious about making the changes that will stop verbal abuse, you will need help. Do not be afraid to face this fact. Needing help does not mean you are inadequate—only that you are wise enough to understand the immense power of old habits. A trusted friend, a professional counselor, and your own faith in God are excellent sources of help. Use them!

5. Be persistent. Changes are hard to make. After making some progress, our common tendency is to slip back into the old habits. Many times you will feel that it's no use. You may be tempted to give up the efforts. Do not give in to such temptations! You must stick with your plan. A helper is especially valuable during these times of temptation. Don't forget to ask for encouragement when you falter.

A psychiatrist friend of mine says he has found that it takes about one month of concentrated effort for every year an old habit has been unchallenged to effect a permanent change. If you are already in the middle years of your life, you may need several years of effort before the new habits become automatic and the old are truly broken. With concentrated effort, you may succeed more quickly, of course, but do not give up. The struggle is worth it!

✦ ✦ ✦

Study Questions

1. What good qualities about yourself can you already identify? In what other ways can you begin to build positive self-esteem?

2. Which of your own needs and emotions can you verbalize? What plan do you have for meeting these needs? Do you still feel like a helpless victim?

3. Describe instances when you have practiced healthy assertiveness. What were the results?

4. In what ways have you unconsciously invited verbal abuse by playing the victim role?

5. Do you have the courage to change your own behavior and stop taking the abuse? Have you given yourself permission to change? What plan do you have to implement these changes?

6. Who do you know who could serve as a support and help in this process? In what ways would you want them to help?

SIXTEEN

Abuse and Addiction

✦ ✦ ✦

VERBAL ABUSE CAN BE MORE CLEARLY UNDERSTOOD if we compare it to other habits such as the abuse of alcohol and drugs which are well known to most Americans. Such abuses have long been known as addictions. And the most successful treatment for all addictions has been developed through the well-known "Anonymous" programs.

Alcoholic's Anonymous (A.A.) was founded in 1934. This program is based on the ultimate dependence of the alcoholic on God, as best the member understands him. Working it successfully demands utmost honesty, openness, and trust in one's fellow members. In 1989, there were 43,107 A.A. groups in the United States, with close to 900,000 members. Some years after A.A. began, the success rate among the 12,000 members at that time was about fifty percent—success being defined as never relapsing into the use of alcohol. Nearly sixty years after its founding, the success rate has dropped to about six percent. Even so, A.A. has the greatest success of any method of treating alcoholism.

Verbal abuse can accurately be defined as another type of addiction. It is addiction to *power*, acquired at the high cost of denigrating others, and is repeated in predictable and definable ways over years of time. Such ongoing abuse produces a growing sense of callousness to the pain of its victims. The continuation of such negative behavior, despite clear information about the pain inflicted on others, describes the seriousness of its pathology.

We will consider the way to find healing if you are purely a victim of verbal abuse. And we must also clarify how to stop the practice of being an abuser. To a significant degree, *abuser and victim become entwined.* Therefore, the solutions to both situations are also closely related.

Let's begin with the explanation and adaptation of the tried and true Twelve Step Program. These are stated as the members of any addictive group would phrase them.

STEP ONE

The first step is this: *We admitted we were powerless over alcohol, that our lives had become unmanageable.* If you are a habitual abuser of negative verbiage, like it or not, you are *powerless* over that practice. I know the reverse seems to be more accurate. You feel very *powerful* when you are lashing out at someone. But remember this is false power, deceptively strong. Underneath is the weakness of the "bully" that prompts such actions.

You have almost certainly recognized at times the hurt and fear in the eyes of your victims. There have undoubtedly been many times when you vowed to stop such cruel words, but inevitably slipped back into those habits. If you recognize these facts as true for you, then you have completed Step One. You know your life in this area of verbal abuse is unmanageable by you.

If you are a victim of abuse, your addictive patterns are a bit different. You have developed the pattern of feeling guilty and anxious. When you feel you have made mistakes or merited the disapproval of another person, you will find some way to communicate with them. You are likely to await the abuse you have always encountered from that person and may even trigger its expression. Afterward, you will feel relieved. It's over! And that sense of temporary relief is your payoff—that which keeps you trapped in your victim role.

You, too, can be free if you recognize your needs and follow these steps:

1. Collect accurate information. You do not need abuse to correct mistakes and restore good feelings. Verbal lashings during your childhood did help relieve your guilt for misdeeds. But it did so at the cost of low self-esteem and high anxiety.
2. When you do anything wrong, simply admit it, make it right, and determine to avoid doing it again. Then forgive yourself and put it behind you.
3. If you feel anxious regarding others' opinions of you, find someone with whom you can discuss that situation. An obective viewpoint can help you see whether you were seriously at fault or your abuser is wrong in his or her judgment. Even when you are the one in error, you do not deserve abuse! Correction is always helpful, but only when it is positive.
4. Fight your temptation to unconsciously seek verbal punishment in order to feel better.
5. Begin to enjoy your life, free of fear and no longer needing or absorbing abuse.
6. Trust God to forgive and accept you.

STEP TWO

We came to believe that a Power greater than ourselves could restore us to sanity. A great many people stumble over Step Two. They have never experienced any positive power greater than themselves. Remember that verbal abusers grew up being abused themselves. The strongest force in their lives was a destructive, painful one. Once they have reached a position of seeming power themselves, they naturally prefer to believe there is no Power beyond their own. If there were,

these abuse victims would fear more abuse and re-experi-
ence their frightened powerlessness.

To master this step, then, demands these four sub-steps:

1. Separate your past and all the abusive people in it from
   the present.
2. Open your mind and emotions to know and feel new
   facts and experiences. The people who caused you so
   much pain are not the only ones in the world.
3. Risk the exploration of this "Power greater than ourselves" who is God, our heavenly father—unique, positive, and always non-abusive!
4. You may mistakenly picture God like you would an abusive father. You need to learn more about God's true
   nature and very personal love for you.

Once you recognize the possibility that such a Power
exists, you will be ready to discover sanity. One severely
abused adolescent said that her mother's tongue-lashings
rarely made sense to her. The lectures were totally dispropor-
tionate to the events on which they focused. At first she
really believed she was crazy. Finally, she came to see her
mother as unbalanced. Sanity was missing in her home life.
God can indeed restore sanity to our lives!

STEP THREE

*We made a decision to turn our will and our lives over to the care
of God as we understood Him.* When we truly come to believe in
the loving, protective qualities of God, then it makes perfect
sense to trust in his care for our lives. To completely turn
over your will and your very life to God demands that you
perceive that as safe. So take some time here. How can you
explore God? There are many ways, but here are some I have
found helpful.

Nature. As I see the lavish beauty and unbelievable harmony
in nature, I cannot fail to see God, the Power infinitely

beyond me. I am speaking here, of course, about nature as the Creator made it, not as people have marred it!

Science. As I have discovered the precision of the laws of physics, chemistry, and biology, I know that a genius had to put it all together. The patterns of the solar system and the exactness of atomical structures, alike, are proof of an intelligence that is immeasurable.

People. While I have shared the horrors of humanity's cruelty to their fellows, I have also been inspired by the heroism of altruistic people. Corrie ten Boom and her Dutch family risked torture and death to save the lives of Jewish people hunted by the Nazis. Corrie and her sister were themselves imprisoned, deprived, and even tortured by that cruel regime. History, ancient and current, is replete with similar examples. Indeed, I believe, God can be seen in such people.

Within myself. Again and again in life, I have hit tough times. Often I had no answers and no resources for coping with those challenges. When I have remembered God and called on the inexhaustible resource of his power, the direction and solutions have been there when I needed them. I only had to ask and listen!

God is far too big for any of us to know him in his entirety, but we can learn much about him. Above all, we can know his love for each one of us personally! God's loving acceptance of you needs to be the foundation of accepting yourself. Once you master this truth, you will be ready to stop so desperately needing the acceptance of your abuser—who is incapable of giving that anyway!

STEP FOUR

We made a searching and fearless moral inventory of ourselves. It is difficult for most people to take this step because they want to be perfect. From earliest childhood, they seek diligently for approval from others—parents, teachers, peers, employers, and families. When people inevitably fail to achieve the perfection such approval often demands, they have only three avenues of recourse:

1. To give up and settle for being not okay.
2. To try heroically to become better, but feeling they can never really make it.
3. To rationalize that whatever they are doing is, after all, okay or at least excusable.

Both verbal abusers and victims tend toward the last choice. They excuse themselves, give in to feelings of helplessness, and somehow manage to remain in the same defeating habits they've always known. Yet these people also live in inner conflict. On one hand, they try to convince themselves that what they are doing is right. But on the other hand, a small voice inside reminds them that their habits are damaging—*not* right.

This conflict between truth and dishonesty consumes a great deal of energy and keeps people stuck in their helplessness. To escape this defeating lifestyle demands the courage to face yourself honestly, searching deeply within yourself, unafraid to discover even the worst of flaws. Only through such discoveries can you change and grow.

STEP FIVE

We admitted to God, to ourselves, and to another human being, the exact nature of our wrongs. In Step Four you learned how important it is to become honest with yourself—to escape the ongoing tug-of-war between rationalizing destructive behaviors and facing up to the defects that cause these.

Step Five clearly demands more. You must learn to trust positive people. As an abuse victim—who may have become an abuser!—you have learned to count on being hurt and victimized. Anticipating the unconditional acceptance this step implies is like learning a new language.

You may believe God will strike you dead if you admit the terrible wrongs you have done. Once again, I urge you to muster the courage to explore who God really is. Only when you come to terms with his grace, love, forgiveness, and power to enable you to change, can you risk this step. The persistent *unwillingness* to be honest and to make changes is what truly provokes God's terrible anger.

Recently I worked with a young woman who had been extremely abused in her early childhood. She experienced ritual torture in the cultish rites of Satan-worship and came to believe that evil power was the only force in existence. As I described to her the love of a healthy father and mother, her face reflected total disbelief. Such love did not exist for her.

Perhaps you, too, have known verbal abuse so extreme that it robbed you of any hope for another way of life. Here is good news for you! There is a better way. Keep working with God—who is the way, the truth, and the life!

It is one thing to be honest with yourself and even with God. After all, he is invisible. It is quite another to trust a human being with your most heinous sins. The people you have known best have habitually hurt you. How, then, can you reveal to a flesh-and-blood person the hidden, dark secrets of your habits?

To complete this step is vital to the process of building a positive relationship based on trust instead of fear. You really must do this. But let me urge you to proceed with caution. Search among everyone you know for a person who is trustworthy. Observe him or her in communication with others and see how they react under stress.

If you can find a human being who remains even-tempered, kind, and unconditionally accepting, seek a block of time with that person. Explain your search and simply ask if she or he is willing to help you with this step. It may be that you will develop a mutual friendship that will last. But if not, even this limited experience will help you to change and will enable you to recognize positive people in building future relationships.

STEP SIX

We were entirely ready to have God remove all these defects of character. To understand this step, you must recognize that the change we are talking about is not simply modifying the patterns of abuse or victimization. Stopping those habits is certainly crucial. But the change, to be effective, must reach deep within your very personality. You must stop being passive if you are to quit being a victim. And you will have to learn self-control and gentle strength in order to quit abusing people.

To make such incisive changes is not only difficult but frighteningly painful. The very core of your being will be shaken and broken. You will experience panic as you realize that you don't know who you will become. To face such fear, of course, demands not only honesty and courage but the knowledge that God's loving hand guides the instrument that will drain the poisons of your past.

You must reach the point of desperation, however, before you will be ready for God's incision. To be "entirely ready," you must understand there is no other way you can know wholeness and health. Do not be afraid of the pain—the healing is certain. And the exuberance of the total health you have never before known will be a marvelous experience for you!

STEP SEVEN

We humbly asked Him to remove our shortcomings. Through the ages, much has been written and taught about humility. Some of you believe it to be an attitude of servility or groveling. If you believe that, you will, of course, not want to walk this step.

But the quality of humility or humbleness is best reflected in the Latin root word, *humilis.* This word originally referred to the ground or earth. Healthy humbleness, then, is basic, earthy, and simple. It demands absolute honesty. I cannot remove my own shortcomings just as I can't take out my own infected appendix. I need a Power beyond my own.

In such a simple, forthright fashion, I come to God admitting my limits, and equally expressing my confidence in his great and loving skill. I know he cares about me and wants to operate on me to correct the defects and restore the function of total health. I humbly submit to this gracious healer!

STEP EIGHT

We made a list of all persons we had harmed, and became willing to make amends to them all. Now we are talking about a truly tough assignment. In Step Seven, you learned to be honest with yourself, God, and one carefully selected other person. This step, solidly built upon the last, is quite another matter! How can you go to all the people whom you have hurt and make things right with them? Even more difficult is the step of going to those who have hurt you and confronting them. You can do it, if you believe!

Step Eight prepares you for doing just that. At this point, of course, you are getting ready for the action, but to work toward actually accomplishing that goal demands total honesty now. If you are the abuser, you must look at people who are closest to you, and thereby are the most threatening to you. Can you honestly say to each of those persons, "I am sorry I hurt you. All this time I've closed my eyes to my wrong-doing. I pretended I was being frank and honest in trying to make *you* better. But now I see I was only fooling *myself*—trying to act smart and strong when I was really foolish and weak!"

How can you make amends to your victims? They will certainly have a hard time accepting mere words as proof of remorse and change. You will need to think of ways to show your victims that you mean business, that you really have changed.

If you are a habitual victim, you may understandably believe you do not need this step. But let me remind you. If you continually allow people to abuse you in a martyrish fashion even as an adult, you have a different role to play, too. To allow others to behave in a mean, hurtful manner— *without even a challenge*—is passively giving consent to their abuse and wrong in itself.

It may seem both undesirable and impossible to confront your abuser. But your words may become a mirror enabling them to see their harshness and even cruelty. Whether your abuser changes is up to that person and God. You can only choose to change yourself—and taking this step of speaking up will demonstrate your growth toward healthy strength.

Certainly you need to be cautious in the way you go about this, but some assertiveness on your part will benefit both you and your abuser. "I am your sister. Remember? All of my life I've allowed you to control me and many times I have felt extremely hurt by your attitude and words. I realize now that this situation is partly my fault. Let me tell you how I'm changing. I will always listen to you and learn from your ideas. But I will no longer allow your words to hurt me. If I start to feel put down and see that my ideas and feelings are disregarded, I will leave the conversation—not because I'm angry, but because I believe you are too good a person to treat anyone in such a way, and I'm too good to deserve such treatment." Naturally, you will use your own words, but perhaps this quote will help to guide your own thoughts.

Making amends is not easy nor can you be certain the other person will accept your efforts. It is an action that only you can initiate, and it must be done honestly and kindly. You are responsible only for your side of this step. Don't worry about the response from others. Do be persistent, however. All good changes take time.

STEP NINE

We made direct amends to such people whenever possible, except when to do so would injure them or others. This is the action step you were preparing for in Step Eight. Once you have swallowed your false pride, have become profoundly honest, and discovered how important this action is, you are ready for some "how to's."

Analyze each individual on your list. Consider the sort of relationship you now have with him or her. Is there some trust and love to balance the negatives? Has this been a relationship full of retaliation that could prompt you to fear being misunderstood and hurt all over again? Or does this person fear you so much that she or he would not believe your apology? I suggest you write out some of your ideas and emotions about each person.

With your mental picture developing, sketch in the best possible setting for your conversation. Try to avoid just taking the easiest way out and consider your options:

1. A telephone call may be best with some individuals. Both of you may speak more frankly and effectively in this way.
2. A carefully written letter may be the only way to reach some people. You may have a friend review it to see if it feels genuine and not hurtful.
3. Going out for lunch or coffee with one to whom you need to make amends offers good advantages. The social setting places healthy controls on both of you. If possible, your generosity in paying the bill is tangible evidence of making amends, as well as a friendly gesture.
4. A visit to the other's home requires careful consideration. The warmth of their own territory may enable the other person to feel more secure. By asking for a visit in the other home, you are evidencing your vulnerability and sincerity. If, however, there is too much activity there, you may lack the necessary privacy. Interruptions at the wrong time can lose the irreplaceable moment!
5. A place of business, yours or theirs, rarely offers the proper setting. This is especially true if your "other" is someone with whom you work. Be sure you do not impose on the other's work and convenience.

6. Your own home may be just the setting you need. You can offer hospitality, plan for privacy, and feel more secure yourself. Be careful to avoid any appearance of "buying" the other's forgiveness.

Whatever the setting, just be sure you carry out your plan. You could wait so long for the right time and place that it just never happens. Do whatever you must to finish this step. I do recommend that you rehearse just a bit how you will say what you need to express. You can do this in your mind, by notes on paper, conversationally in front of a mirror, or in a dialogue with a friend. Again, avoid sounding like an actress, but knowing what you wish to say will help.

Above all, be genuine. And at all costs, avoid defensiveness. If the other person attacks or accuses you, agree with him/her. You are in this to set things right and to make amends—not to make yourself seem righteous!

STEP TEN

We continued to take personal inventory and when we were wrong, promptly admitted it. The habits of a lifetime are not easy to break. Nor is it easy to quickly develop new ones. If you are caught in the habits of being victimized by verbal abuse, changing will demand constant effort over months of time. The same holds true for the one who is an abuser.

Remember, one month of work is usually required to change the habits of one year of your life's old patterns. So you can see that even the intensity and thoroughness of the first nine steps are not enough. You need to invest constant follow-through and repetition—the ongoing practice of *daily* inventories and corrections—to stop abuse.

Many years ago, I took this step myself. I made a commitment that every evening I would review my day and my actions. If I discovered any hurts I had inflicted or felt, I refused to retire until I had made amends and cleared away misunderstandings. I have found it to be a great way to live.

STEP ELEVEN

We sought through prayer and meditation to improve our conscious contact with God as we understood Him, praying only for the knowledge of His will for us and the power to carry that out. This profound statement needs no further comment, except the exhortation to practice it. A new way of life opens up for all addicts who give up practicing their old routines and seek out the guidance of God. It is exciting to discover the One who enables us to transcend old patterns by providing new Power!

STEP TWELVE

Having had a spiritual awakening as a result of these steps, we tried to carry this message to alcoholics [or to victims and abusers] and to practice these principles in all our affairs. Recently I visited with an aging man who had greatly influenced me in years past. As we reminisced, he reminded me of the first thirty-five years of his life. He stated, "I was so bad, I can't begin to describe it—how bad it really was."

I found it almost impossible to believe this man, now so mellow with the wisdom of some eighty years. But because of his integrity, I knew he spoke the truth. He offers visible evidence of the success of these twelve steps. I had heard him describe the struggle he went through to achieve each upward tread. It had not been an easy journey. But the pain he had known, he said, was nothing compared to the peace he now enjoys, every day. You, too, can know such peace!

✦ ✦ ✦

Study Questions

1. As a victim of verbal abuse, in what ways do you feel emotionally intertwined with your abuser?

2. If you are verbally abusive, how do you experience the deceptive sense of power it produces? Have you been *pow-erless* over this addictive habit?

3. As the victim of verbal abuse, how do you see this pattern in your own behavior: feeling guilty and anxious over some perceived shortcomings, communicating about them with your abuser, waiting or triggering the deserved abuse, and then feeling a temporary sense of *relief* as your payoff?

4. Describe your image of God. Do you see him as an abusive father? How have you experienced his loving acceptance? How can you remember to draw upon his power when you feel powerless?

5. In what ways are you driven by a need to be perfect in order to gain the approval of others? In what ways have you been quick to justify your own negative behavior and project blame onto your abuser?

6. Have you ever confronted your abuser? If so, describe what happened.

SEVENTEEN

Doing Something about It

✦ ✦ ✦

F EW WORDS HAVE SUCH PROFOUND MEANING in the context
of wholeness and health as does the word *"forgiveness."*
All too often this concept has been over-simplified or totally
rejected as being merely a religious term. Forgiveness is a
process that can be agonizing, torturously slow in its progress. Yet it must be understood and practiced if the power
of past abuse is to be broken.

Many people I know seem to believe that forgiveness is a
simple statement based on an often flimsy decision. The forgiveness I am describing is not that shallow. It begins, in fact,
with the acknowledgment of pain. Many victims of verbal
abuse have grown calloused—understandably so.

People can absorb only so much pain and then they will
deny it, ignore it, and hide it away in the depths of their
memories—a process referred to as repression. It seems less
painful to rationalize away the hurts, feel angry, or even
worse, indifferent, toward the abuser.

Such efforts to deal with pain, however, are like putting a
tiny Band-Aid on a big boil or abscess. In order to heal such
an infected wound, the poison must be drained, allowing

wholeness to be restored from the inside. So to even begin this healing process of forgiving others demands admitting the hurt, and in some degree, even reliving it.

One woman with whom I worked had suffered major verbal abuse from her father. Natalie had genuinely tried to let go of her ancient trauma, but one by one the painful scenes from long ago popped up to renew the old anguish she had known so well. She remembered hiding with her tears and her pain under a table near her father's desk. Even as an adult, the shame and helplessness Natalie had endured under his wrath horrified her. But she heroically endured that remembered pain and found permanent healing.

LEARNING TO FORGIVE

Here are the procedures that have repeatedly brought such "inside-out" healing to abuse victims with whom I have worked over the years. In essence, these steps encompass four vital stages of forgiveness.

1. Experience, once more, the pain you knew. Whether you are the victim, the abuser, or both, you felt some variation of pain. Allow your memories of that pain to motivate you to take the next action step.

2. Collect information. The last thing you probably *feel* like doing is spending time gathering information about a person who has hurt you. Nevertheless, that is what you must do if you are ever to become free of this pain. The facts you need are those that relate to reasons for that abuse. Through relatives, diaries, photo albums, or friends, find out all you can about anyone who may have wounded you.

Try to unearth additional information about your own childhood as well.

a. What were you like as a small child?
b. Whom, among the entire family, did you resemble?

    c. What were you like in those years before you can re-
       member?

    d. What role did *you* play in the events of your abuse—
       even though you didn't realize it? Be careful to avoid
       blaming yourself with this question. At this point we're
       just seeking information!

3. Allow the information to become understanding. If you are
willing to expend such energy, you may discover some extremely useful insights. It may be that you have uncanny
resemblances to some relative like your grandfather or aunt,
for example. Your abuser may, ever so unwittingly, have transferred to you the pain and resentment they once experienced with those people.

That information does not excuse the abuse of which you
were the victim, but it can help you to understand it better.
You can see that you were not really a bad person. Hopefully
with that awareness, you may be more magnanimous and
ready to forgive those who have hurt you so badly.

4. Exert your will. The next action you will need to take is
one of your will. You may understand ever so clearly the defects in your abuser, but you may still cling to your hurts and
resentments because of the apparent emotional protection
these feelings provide. For example, even a little bit of anger
toward someone keeps you from being so vulnerable to further hurts they may inflict.

It is most tempting to prefer anger to forgiveness. But pro-
longed anger will create deep bitterness in you and even predispose you to become an abuser youself. And your anger
may not have any positive impact on that other person at all.
It is totally wasted! You must decide: what sort of person will
you choose to be?

If you decide to be a healthy, loving human being, you
must forgive. And your willpower is required to do this.
"Aha!" you may say. "Now I know why Mother was so critical
of me. Every time she looked at me, she saw Grandpa. And I

realize now how much he had abused her. It wasn't really me she was after." If you truly understand the dynamics involved here, you are ready to make that freeing choice to let go of the past and completely forgive.

In a workshop I attended many years ago, the leader demonstrated how one may totally relinquish old feelings. He asked one of the members who was struggling with the pain of his old abuse to follow these simple directions. "Dwight," he requested, "take out your pocket handkerchief. Now wad it up and hold it tightly in your hand. Hold it very close for several minutes."

Dwight obediently followed these instructions. After some time, the leader returned his attention to Dwight. "How does your hand feel now?" he asked. All of us could identify with this man. His hand was pale and obviously stiff, which is exactly how he described it.

"Now," asked the workshop leader, "open your hand and allow that handkerchief to drop." With evident effort, Dwight opened his stiff hand, and just as expected, the cloth fell to the floor. Probably none of us in that room will ever forget that object lesson. Dwight broke into tears as he realized the relief of dropping the burden of so many old hurts, just as voluntarily as he had relinquished the handkerchief. A decision of the will is at the crux of this step.

Let me recap these four vital stages of forgiveness:

1. Acknowledge and face the pain all over again. Don't try to minimize it or hide it.
2. Collect as much information as possible about the abusive episodes from your past. Try to do this objectively and fairly—be fair to yourself as well as to your abuser.
3. Allow the information to penetrate to your very heart. If it stays only in your mind, the pertinent facts will not effect the forgiveness we're describing.
4. Make a conscious choice, by an act of your will, to totally relinquish all the hurts, fears, and anger of the past. Whenever old resentments return, or you fear further hurts, repeat this act of letting go of these damag-

ing feelings. Meanwhile, enjoy the freedom you will experience through learning to forgive.

HOW TO STOP BEING AN ABUSER

The focus of this book is most clearly aimed at the cessation of your being a victim and at your healing. Learning the steps for healing from the hurts of the past is a complex process, but we have tried to show you how that can be done. You have read, however, that many victims of abuse become verbal abusers themselves. If you fall into this category, there is also great hope for you!

First, you must be honest enough to face yourself squarely. Few people really *want* to be mean, so you have probably tried to be a good, honest, forthright person. In the process of trying to be good, you may have learned to twist your thinking just enough to convince yourself that you are not abusive. You may see yourself as merely blunt, frank, or forthright. You perhaps have said to anyone who has confronted you, "I'm simply outspoken. I've always been this way and you have to accept me as I am. If you can't take honesty, you'd better look at yourself!"

Such an attitude is extremely common among verbal abusers. They are quick to justify themselves, projecting all the blame for personal hurts on the other person. In the short run, this kind of thinking gives them power and convinces them they are okay, while you are not. In the long run, of course, verbal abusers must face the truth—that they are often unfair or even cruel.

Such a revelation creates intense remorse and guilt. You can do one of two things about these painful feelings:

1. *Deny them.* By using old habits, you can once more convince yourself that you are not really an abusive person. Doing so will sear your conscience and entrench you even more deeply in the rut of your abusive patterns. But you will feel somewhat better.

2. *Allow them to motivate you to change.* Remember that real guilt and remorse can be your very best friends. The pain they create can move you to recognize where you are at fault and how you need to be different. By facing up to your cruelty, you can learn to eliminate it.

Going around hurting people's feelings is absolutely wrong. You need to recognize your culpability. To do so demands healthy bluntness—with yourself. You've been good at being "blunt" with others (abusive is more accurate). Now practice basic honesty and frankness on yourself! (But without abuse!)

Obviously I hope you will make the second choice above. At the risk of berating or abusing yourself, sit down and face the facts. Use honest, real words as you think. For example, stop calling your abusiveness by those complimentary terms—like "open," "frank," and "forthright." Instead, open your mind to the facts of your behavior. You have been "cruel," "mean," "hurtful," "demeaning," and wrong!

Self-abuse would next call for some act of punishing yourself. Some people punish themselves by getting sick. Others depress themselves and use negative feelings to spoil all their pleasure. Still others withdraw in isolation and moodiness, unwittingly hurting those around them even more! Don't use any of these ineffective measures!

Here are some useful steps you can take. These will work—if you work them!

1. Be grateful for your discovery. If you had chosen to ignore the truth, you could have gone on forever hurting people near you. Recently I spoke with an adolescent who told me about his grandmother. "She was really mean!" he stated. Now I've known some "mean" parents, and often commend their "meanness" if that implies tough love!

But further exploration revealed that this grandmother was indeed mean. She had verbally and physically abused her large family so severely that all but one grew up with major problems. Contrary to most doting grandparents, she had carried on her abusive treatment to the next generation.

One of her children, however, was fortunate enough to recognize the abuse in her painful words and how they had injected poison into the lives of that family. This adult daughter finally refused to follow the pattern and became a sort of haven to her siblings and their children. She learned how to change—and so can you if you will allow yourself to endure the initial shock and hurt of your discovery.

2. Explore the cause of your habit. It's not enough to believe you are abusive just because your parents were. You also need to inventory your own personality. Only when you can define the traits that make you a likely candidate for the title "verbal abuser" can you effectively break the habit. The following questions will be helpful in such an effort.

    a. Do you feel weak and inadequate except when you are angry and lash out at others with words?

    b. Do you allow stress to build up until it bursts the boundaries of your controls?

    c. Are you one of those many people who never mastered the skill of self-control?

    d. Do you even believe it is foolish to practice this time-honored art?

    e. Do you believe it is desirable and honest to express feelings and ideas with all the intensity you happen to experience?

    f. Do you use anger against others to protect yourself from being vulnerable?

    g. Are you aware that you often find low self-esteem to be the core of your personality?

3. Recognize your strengths. Most of us are far more capable than we ever realize. You have already discovered your weaknesses. Now look for your assets. By your very choice of being honest, you have laid the strong cornerstone of change. Without honesty, no insight or lasting changes can be accomplished.

Among our most precious assets are our mental capacity and our will-power. Most of us fail to use our brains to the maximum, but you can think, reason, and make wise choices, as well as you did wrong ones. It just takes practice. You also have the priceless gift of a will. It may be weak at times, but you can develop those magic muscles of willpower by putting them to use. One way to practice positive willpower is to make yourself do one thing everyday that you hate doing. And stop yourself daily from doing one thing you want very much to do. Exerting your strong, positive will is the ultimate answer to breaking bad habits.

4. Practice the rules for change. Earlier in Chapter 15, we listed five common sense steps for change. Review them and practice using them. Remember to enjoy your successes along the way. The process of change is so tedious, you will often be tempted to give up.

To overcome this temptation, remember how miserable you felt after an episode of abusing someone. And keep in focus the contrasting good feelings you get when you handle situations in a loving, positive way. As you experience even occasional successes, they will encourage you. You can anticipate a whole new life style even as you change and grow!

HEALTHY COMMUNICATION SKILLS

Once you have broken the old patterns of behavior and speech, you will need to focus on creating new ones. You may need to search for some role models. Observe the interactions of others. You can learn from both positive and negative examples.

Once in a while, you may find on TV or in a movie a really good interaction in which abuse could have been perpetrated but wasn't. How did the actors avoid abuse? And when you do observe abuse, as happens so often, how does it evolve? Such habits of observation and analysis can teach you brand new communications skills.

Since verbal abuse is certainly one form of communicating, let's explore some basics of good skills in this crucial area. Unfortunately, *most* people communicate the same way they do other things of an interpersonal nature. They just *do* it. Impulsively and reactively, folks blunder their way through life practicing poor communication.

The concepts needed to correct such old habits are simple to grasp. They are not even difficult to practice. It is breaking the old familiar patterns that is truly difficult. Great communicators utilize the following four skills.

1. They are committed to accuracy and honesty. In any conversation they *think* before they speak and they strive to express themselves understandably, briefly, and accurately. They may weave in a touch of humor and even practice the strength of gentleness, as well.

In transactions with others, good communicators strive to *hear* as accurately as they speak. How easy it is to focus so intently on one's next comments that one fails to listen to the other person! To correct that tendency, your will-power comes in handy. Will yourself to listen to the speaker. If you aren't sure you are understanding them correctly, stop the interaction. Try a statement like, "Jim, did I hear you right? Here's what I thought you said. Is that correct?"

Many misunderstandings could be completely avoided if we made it a practice to check out the meanings of others' words. Once you discover the other person did not intend to hurt you verbally, you are not likely to impulsively retaliate. Thus one more step is accomplished in breaking your abusive habits.

2. They stick with kindliness and grace. Harsh, abusive words stop positive communication and create fear, anger, withdrawal, or aggression—or even all of these simultaneously.

To break the habit of abuse, you must practice the art of graciousness. By defining and insuring the accurate exchange of information, much of the natural tendency to bristle and react to each other abusively is gone.

3. Listen to and observe emotions as well as ideas. The basic meaning of words can be quite different in the light of various emotions that are woven into the ideas they express. Learn to identify the many rich shades of feelings in your communications. First, identify your own emotions. Anxiety, fear, worry, sadness, and caution all belong to the vulnerable part of you. Irritation, frustration, rage, and fury are manifestations of your angry, aggressive nature. Tenderness, compassion, gentleness, and yearning are expressions of your love.

Once you recognize these feelings in yourself, you can more easily identify them in others. You need to understand and recall that aggressive emotions cover up tender, vulnerable, painful emotions. You will have developed a great asset in breaking your patterns of abuse when you find the strength to own, express, and ask help for your tender emotions. You will no longer need the false protection of anger.

When you read another person's emotions accurately, you will inevitably discover that some hurt or fear underlies any verbal attack or anger. Once you recognize these tender emotions, you are not likely to want to retaliate. And once you find your own vulnerable feelings, you will be more able to protect them in healthy ways rather than disguising them through abuse.

Often our best protection against hurting others or being abused is the very open revelation of our own vulnerability. I discovered this concept through a book about wild animals entitled *King Solomon's Ring*, but I cannot find either the book or its author. Let me explain how this principle can work. This story focused on the natural habits of animals of prey. They would rarely kill one of their own species and resorted to killing another species only out of hunger or self-protection. They would, however, fight each other at times.

Such creatures fought to win a mate or to gain certain power within their group.

The person who so carefully observed these magnificent animals discovered an unusual action that prevented death. When one male animal found that he was losing the fight with another and could not go on, he would inevitably cease his efforts. Simultaneously, he would stretch out his neck to one side, deliberately exposing his vital jugular vein. His opponent could have slashed that vein and caused immediate death. But that did not happen. The conqueror would recognize that simple motion as a sign of giving up and would walk away.

To save your own emotional health, you may need to practice a similar act of vulnerability. By exhibiting the courage and wisdom to withdraw from a destructive interaction and reveal your tender side, you actually will win the altercation! Frankly, such an act of capitulation requires and demonstrates much greater strength than practicing abuse.

4. They read body language well. In the interest of following the steps above, good communication is facilitated by learning careful observation. Because so many people have not learned the benefit of vulnerability, they practice cover-ups. They try to act tough instead of revealing their fear or worry and inevitably behave rudely—when in fact they feel hurt or embarrassed.

If you will observe carefully, you are quite likely to uncover the hidden, true feelings of another. First, look at the person's entire posture. Is he or she tense and erect or relaxed and bent? Next, watch the hands and arms. Are they flexed and taut as if ready to strike in anger, or held out in a gesture of helplessness or pleading? Observe the face. Is the overall expression one of sadness, anxiety, anger, joy, or concern?

Someone has said, "Eyes are the window of the soul." I certainly agree. Even the most calloused persons cannot totally disguise their feelings as expressed by the eyes. How often I have found access to an angry adolescent's real, vulnerable feelings by reading those expressive eyes. The mist of unshed tears, the wistfulness of grief, the twinkle of a half-buried sense of healthy humor, are all visible in the eyes.

The set of the jaw and mouth are the last major focus as you train your mental camera on body language. A tightly set jaw and pursed lips depict anger and resistance. A loose jaw and trembling lips usually reveal sadness or depression. Lips that curl in scorn or cynicism are all too easily read, and the gentle smile of good humor is refreshing to see.

All of these observations may seem unrelated to verbal abuse. But in fact, they are vitally important in stopping any abusive habits you may have developed. As you know and understand yourself and others better, you gain the strength of awareness that will enable you to give up your abusive behavior. You can become so loving and secure, you will no longer need to shore up your sagging ego.

Those of us who have suffered the anguish of verbal abuse would love to see those habits changed. We would like to enjoy a world that is safe, an environment that allows for risks and mistakes, surroundings that promote correction by encouragement and hope for success, and the opportunity to offer and seek the healing of forgiveness.

Such a world may seem impossible in this era of self-serving narcissism. But your individual sector of the world will change for the better when you understand the concepts in this book and practice them. I wish for each of you a safe and wonderful world.

✦ ✦ ✦

Study Questions

1. How would you define forgiveness?

2. What specific memories do you have of the pain from verbal abuse? If you have repressed a lot of the pain from past verbal abuse, are you *willing* to admit the hurt, relive the pain, drain the wound of poisons, and be healed from the inside?

3. What role did *you* play in your abuse?

4. What insights have you gained from gathering information about your abuser? How have these insights penetrated your heart?

5. Are you ready to *let go* of your pain, fear, resentment, and anger? Can you *choose to forgive* your abuser as an act of your will?

6. In what ways has your own behavior been cruel or unfair? How does that make you feel? Are you tempted to rationalize, punish yourself, or withdraw in isolation and moodiness?

7. What vulnerable and painful emotions are you attempting to cover over by verbal abuse? What are some healthier ways to protect those vulnerable feelings, and even express your vulnerability as a pathway to intimacy?

Support Group
for Victims of Verbal Abuse
Twelve-Week Guide

THIS APPENDIX OFFERS GUIDELINES for someone wishing to start a support group for victims of verbal abuse using this book as a teaching tool. The twelve-week schedule gives ample time for group members to understand the area of verbal abuse and begin to work through some of the surrounding emotional issues. The questions at the end of each chapter can be used as homework assignments. Keep in mind that some flexibility may be needed to accommodate individual group dynamics.

WEEK 1
Chapter One

Topic: What is verbal abuse?
    a. personal introductions by those present and their reasons for attending this support group
    b. common ingredients of verbal abuse
    c. working toward a simple definition
    d. the repetitive pattern of verbal abuse

WEEK 2
Chapters Two and Three

Topic: Verbal abuse in marriage and child-rearing
    a. verbal abuse as a power struggle

b. common areas of marital arguments
c. vulnerability and intimacy in family life
d. the impact of childhood verbal abuse on sexuality
e. abusive forms of discipline or training

WEEK 3
Chapters Four and Five

Topic: Sibling and transgenerational verbal abuse
a. damaged self-worth and lowered self-esteem
b. life-shaping labels and nicknames
c. jealousy and resentment
d. transgenerational patterns
e. the "time out" approach

WEEK 4
Chapters Six and Seven

Topic: Verbal abuse in academic and religious settings
a. examples of classroom verbal abuse by teachers or students
b. suggestions for correcting such abuse
c. the shame and guilt produced by unrealistic expectations in religious groups
d. power struggles, manipulation, and exclusion
e. positive ways to respond to conflict and abuse

WEEK 5
Chapters Eight and Nine

Topic: Verbal abuse on the job and in the world
a. work environments as influenced from the top down
b. the issue of sexual harassment
c. personal horror stories from traveling, shopping, eating out, or other social occasions
d. being treated as inferior and subservient
e. ways of coping with verbally abusive people

WEEK 6
Chapters Ten and Eleven

Topic: Various forms of verbal abuse
a. cruel humor versus healthy humor

b. manipulation and criticism
c. negative labels and categorizations
d. abusive body language
e. unfavorable comparisons

WEEK 7
Chapter Twelve

Topic: The effects of verbal abuse
  a. ways to rebuild damaged self-esteem
  b. the spectrum of reactions to verbal abuse
  c. limited potential and ways to overcome it
  d. life-shaping predictions and "curses"

WEEK 8
Chapter Thirteen

Topic: How someone becomes a verbal abuser
  a. being the victim of verbal abuse
  b. feeling profoundly powerless and anxious
  c. coping with stress
  d. becoming depressed and exploding in anger

WEEK 9
Chapter Fourteen

Topic: Determining if *you* are an abuser
  a. recognizing if your family and friends are fearful or avoiding you
  b. leaving confrontations feeling guilty or ashamed
  c. elements of healthy confrontation
  d. venting intense negative feelings
  e. anger as a cover-up for fear

WEEK 10
Chapter Fifteen

Topic: Coping with the pain of verbal abuse
  a. restoring a sense of self-worth
  b. understanding your own needs and emotions
  c. assertiveness versus aggression

d. examining how you may have participated in the process of verbal abuse

e. five steps to change

WEEK 11
Chapter Sixteen

Topic: The Twelve Steps and verbal abuse as an addiction

a. powerlessness versus the false sense of power produced by being verbally abusive

b. learning to let go and let God restore you to sanity

c. making a personal inventory of wrongs and admitting them to another person

d. making amends to people you have harmed

e. the Twelve Steps as a way of life

WEEK 12
Chapter Seventeen

Topic: An action plan to combat verbal abuse

a. healing from the inside out

b. four stages of forgiveness

c. how to stop being an abuser

d. healthy communication skills

Bibliography

Baily, T.F., and Baily, W.H. *Operational Definitions of Child Emotional Maltreatment.* Final Report of a Federal Project. Augusta, Maine, 1986.

Call, J.D., Galenson, E., Tyson, R.L. *Frontiers of Infant Psychiatry.* New York: Basic Books, Inc., 1983.

Clark, Jean Illsley and Dawson, Connie. *Growing up Again.* San Francisco: Harper & Row, 1989.

Garbarino, J., Guttmann, E., Seeley, J.W. *The Psychologically Battered Child.* San Francisco: Jossey-Bass Publishers, 1986.

Harris, Thomas Anthony. *I'm OK, You're OK.* New York: Harper & Row, 1969.

May, Rollo. *Power and Innocence: A Search for the Sources of Violence.* New York: C.C. Norton, 1972.

Orwell, George. *1984.* New York: Harcourt, Brace Publishing, 1949, 1974.

Stinnett, Nick and DeFrain, John. *The Secrets of Strong Families.* New York: Berkley Books, 1985.

William Gladden Foundation. *A Parent's Guide to Building Children's Self-Esteem.* New York: The William Gladden Foundation, 1991.

Other Recovery Books of Interest
from Servant Publications

Forgiving Our Parents, Forgiving Ourselves
From the Minirth-Meier Clinic
Dr. David Stoop and Dr. James Masteller

Forgiving Our Parents, Forgiving Ourselves begins by exploring the family patterns that perpetuate dysfunction. Step-by-step, readers will learn to construct a psychological family tree that will help them uncover family secrets and family habits that have profoundly shaped their adult identity.

As they develop greater understanding of their family origin and its effect for good or ill, they will be able to take the essential step of forgiveness. When that happens, they will find themselves moving into a place of profound spiritual healing which will change their lives forever. *$16.99*

Healing Adult Children of Divorce
Taking Care of Unfinished Business So You Can Be Whole Again
Dr. Archibald D. Hart

Often adult children of divorce struggle with fear, shame, anxiety, anger, and disillusionment. They fear failure, suffer low self-esteem, and avoid risks in love and work. Dr. Hart knows from personal as well as professional experience what it means to be an adult child of divorce. He offers not only psychological insight but biblically-based wisdom that is essential to meaningful growth, recovery, and true healing. *$16.99*

Addicted to "Love"
*Recovering from Unhealthy Dependencies
in Romance, Relationships, and Sex*
Stephen Arterburn

Stephen Arterburn describes why sex addiction is on the rise, how it manifests itself in the church and in Christian family life, who it afflicts, and what we can do if we suspect that a spouse, friend, or family member may be suffering from it. *$16.99*

128853